When the construction of Chartres Cathedral, as we know it today, was nearly completed in the early thirteenth century, Guillaume le Breton wrote in his chronicle of the *"countless . . . signs and favors of grace by which the Blessed Virgin shows that the Mother of God has a special love for this one church, granting a minor place, as it were, to all other churches."* Almost 800 years later, Jill Geoffrion explains in this remarkable book why he made this claim. Her commentary and accompanying images help us to understand Mary's roles both in the temporal scheme as Theotokos or "God-bearer," and in the celestial, as Queen of the Saints and Queen of the Angels who serves as the principal intercessor with her Son for humankind. This is an excellently written text, well documented with relevant biblical and exegetic sources, and superbly illustrated with photographic details.

—MALCOLM MILLER, distinguished guide and author of *Chartres Cathedral*

This book is borne out of the personal experience, when the author, a woman, a Protestant pastor, and a mother sat in prayer near the relic of the Veil of the Virgin Mary. Carried by biblical texts and supported by the beautiful and emotionally sensitive photographs of the author, it helps us to discover the traces of Mary, whose presence is found throughout the cathedral. In this quest, Our Lady of Chartres appears as both an exceptional reliquary and a monstrance of Christ and God himself, which Mary helped to reveal. Praise should be given to this work, which through the figure of the Queen of Heaven and through the beauty of her representations at Chartres leads our hearts to her son and his Heavenly Father.

—IRÈNE JOURD'HEUIL, Author and Curator of Historical Monuments of the Regional Department of Cultural Affairs for Central France

This book makes a crucial contribution to the literature devoted to Mary. The author here traces the trajectory of this story beginning with Mary as the Mother of Jesus, continuing with her role as Mother of God and Mother of the Church, all the way to expressions of her importance in contemporary perspective. One finds evidence throughout this beautiful volume of the author's sustained commitment to exploring these Marian themes as they are to be found at Chartres. The text, grounded in solid research, reveals the author's enthusiasm and deeply felt convictions for this material. The superb pictures that grace these pages, together with an exhaustive bibliography and glossary, make this a book to be highly recommended.

—HELGE BURGGRABE, musician and composer of the oratorio commissioned for the Chartres millennial

VISIONS OF MARY

ART, DEVOTION, AND BEAUTY
AT CHARTRES CATHEDRAL

Jill K. H. Geoffrion

VISIONS OF MARY

ART, DEVOTION, AND BEAUTY
AT CHARTRES CATHEDRAL

mount
tabor
BOOKS

PARACLETE PRESS
BREWSTER, MASSACHUSETTS
BARGA, ITALY

2017 First Printing

Visions of Mary: Art, Devotion, and Beauty at Chartres Cathedral

Text and Photographs Copyright © 2017 by Jill Kimberly Hartwell Geoffrion, except where noted.

ISBN: 978-1-61261-894-4

LIBRARY OF CONGRESS CATALOGING-IN-PUBLICATION DATA
Names: Geoffrion, Jill Kimberly Hartwell, 1958- author.
Title: Visons of Mary : art, devotion, and beauty at Chartres Cathedral / The
    Rev. Jill Kimberly Hartwell Geoffrion, PhD.
Description: Brewster, Massachusetts : Paraclete Press Inc., 2017. | Includes
    bibliographical references and index.
Identifiers: LCCN 2017013735 | ISBN 9781612618944 (hardcover dust-jacket)
Subjects: LCSH: Mary, Blessed Virgin, Saint–Art. | Mary, Blessed Virgin,
    Saint–Devotion to. | Cathâedrale de Chartres.
Classification: LCC N8070 .G39 2017 | DDC 704.9/4855–dc23
LC record available at https://lccn.loc.gov/2017013735

10 9 8 7 6 5 4 3 2 1

Published by Paraclete Press
Brewster, Massachusetts, and Barga, Italy
www.paracletepress.com
Printed in China

CONTENTS

Chapter Three:
MARY, MOTHER OF THE CHURCH
53

Chapter Four:
MARY, MOTHER OF US ALL
75

Chapter Five:
MARY AT CHARTRES IN THE TWENTY-FIRST CENTURY
97

Appendix One:
SIGNIFICANT ARCHITECTURAL ELEMENTS OF CHARTRES CATHEDRAL
119

PROLOGUE

In dangers,

in distress,

in uncertainty,

think of Mary,

call upon Mary.

She never leaves your lips,

she never departs from your heart;

and so that you may obtain the help of her prayers,

never forget the example of her life.

If you follow her, you cannot falter;

if you pray to her, you cannot despair;

if you think of her, you cannot err.

If she sustains you, you will not stumble;

if she protects you, you have nothing to fear;

if she guides you, you will never flag;

if she is favorable to you, you will attain your goal.

—BERNARD OF CLAIRVAUX (1090–1153)

The story of Chartres begins not with the marvelous building so familiar to many who come here as pilgrims or tourists. It all began with an angel's surprising visit to a young woman more than two millennia ago, announcing to this daughter of Zion that God had entrusted her with something far beyond what she felt prepared to do: to bear the eternal Word who was to be the Savior of the world. She agreed, often unlike us, saying, "I understand, so I will do it." With a courage we too rarely have, she said "Yes!" to God's work in and through her without understanding. She simply responded: "Let it be to me according to your Word."

Mary is everywhere present in the images found throughout Chartres Cathedral, though never shown as one who sought to draw attention to herself. For she knew that her only vocation was to manifest for us, and share with us, the gift of salvation through the coming of the Word made flesh in and through her, Jesus Christ. She wants us, like the servants at the wedding in Cana, to "Do everything he tells you to do." Actively taking part in God's plan, she lives in familiarity with the Lord, just as each of us who "hear his word, and keep it" are invited to do. This is the story of Mary. It is also and in crucial ways the story of Chartres. And this is to say, it is our story today.

Throughout this cathedral are signs that tell this story, one that grew through the ways people experienced her help, encouragement, and witness over the centuries. This book helps us understand the richness of this testimony. This is a story that begins anew with each generation, as the author of this splendid book helps us see and understand. In the joy of the resurrection of Jesus, Mary was in prayer with the disciples.

She was waiting with them for the Holy Spirit who had come upon her, which would make of them God's "witnesses in Jerusalem, in all Judea and Samaria, and to the ends of the earth."

I thank Jill Geoffrion, author of this witness to Mary, "Our Lady of Chartres." In these pages, she shares with us her passion and insights into the role Mary has played in her life and continues to play in the lives of the faithful. I pray that you will find in this book an invitation to experience the rich devotion of the Church through the ages. May you find in these pages encouragement to join this witness to the grace Our Lady bears for us and for the world of the twenty-first century.

+MICHEL PANSARD, BISHOP OF CHARTRES
Easter, 2017

PREFACE

Here am I, the servant of the Lord;
let it be with me according to your word. (Luke 1:38)

For much of my life, I viewed Mary as a biblical heroine who appeared roughly once a year, during the reading of the Christmas story. My Protestant upbringing helped me to think of her as a historical figure worthy of admiration, as a woman who had said yes to God, during the Annunciation (left). The invitation to search for a wider perspective came in 2008, when I tried to locate and photograph the 175 images of Mary in Chartres Cathedral that the priest and historian Yves Delaporte had identified in his volume *The Three Marys of Chartres Cathedral*. Very quickly, I came face-to-face with my profound ignorance of Mary's significant role in the history of the church.

While working closely with French and American Catholic colleagues at Chartres Cathedral, I was surprised by their devotion to Mary. It was foreign to my experience and interest, but I took it seriously and tried to find out more. Not only were they patient with my questions about the Catholic church's history in relation to Jesus's mother, but also they shared very openly who Mary was to them, and how their theological beliefs informed their understanding of who she had been and who she was.

At Chartres, built and adorned with stained glass and sculpture in thirteenth-century France, Mary is seldom shown alone; her motherhood and discipleship are emphasized. As a mother myself, and as an ordained minister, I found these dimensions of Mary's witness attractive. The more I studied the medieval images of Mary in the cathedral, the more I understood how and why the mother of Jesus came to be honored not only as the biblical mother of Jesus with whom I was familiar but also as the Mother of God, Mother of the Church, and compassionate mother of all, accessible in prayer and helpful in interceding on our behalf. What a surprise!

The Marian images on Delaporte's list, as well as additional images that Alain Pierre Louët and I identified (see pp. 137ff), were the tip of the iceberg of Marian devotion at Chartres. Marian imagery abounds on many of the liturgical items used in the cathedral. Also, there are many overt and subtle Marian symbols both inside and on the outside of the cathedral. The more I learned, the more my mind stretched to fit the pieces together. My heart was opening wider to the possibility of encountering Mary personally too.

While reading recommended historical and devotional texts about Mary that related to the images in Chartres, I came upon a practical suggestion. A French ecumenical group of Protestant, Orthodox, and Catholic scholars and religious leaders, after spending several years studying and discussing Mary, urged Catholic and Orthodox believers to ask Mary to introduce them to her son. They also encouraged Protestants to ask Jesus to introduce them to his mother.

As I began praying to Christ with this request, nothing earth-shattering seemed to happen. I adopted a wait-and-see attitude. A year or so later, I noticed that when I prayed on the benches outside a chapel with beautiful stained glass, most of my prayers were not for world needs or friends' challenges. They were consistently and almost exclusively for my immediate and extended family. Curious about how that location might have influenced my conversations with God, I set out to find out what sort of a chapel it was. Someone explained that it was the Chapel of the Heart of Mary and contained the Veil of Mary, which was something I hadn't noticed until that moment!

"I have never heard that Mary wore a veil," was my initial reaction, followed by a very Protestant, "That's not in the Bible." If I had understood that this piece of cloth considered a relic, I would likely have fled. My ignorance, however, was so large that my American Baptist twenty-first-century sensibilities were not

bothered! I looked at the cloth and thought about how much Mary had loved Jesus. As I focused on my love for my own sons, warmth radiated from my heart through my body and beyond it—as if it were reaching toward the veil. Suddenly, I grasped that Mary was not only my sister in faith as a follower of Jesus, but more specifically my *older* sister, and that motherhood bound us together. I imagined that Mary, wherever and whoever she might be, could understand everything I held in my mother's heart. I looked at that piece of white cloth with gratitude for all who had come to pray near it over the centuries, including women who lived nearby, such as Marguerite of Lèves (left), and those who had traveled thousands of miles. I was aware of swimming with joy and wonder in an ocean of prayers.

"If this is Mary's Veil, then it must have touched Jesus. And if it touched Jesus, then in some mystical way I'm close to him right now, even if he isn't 'here.'" The thought was unexpected. Next, I remembered the deep connection with Jesus that I felt when I visited his "Garden Tomb" in Israel. As I gazed at this cloth that had first-century pollen from the Middle East on it, it no longer seemed to matter whether the veil had been worn by Mary, or had physically touched Jesus. Its ability to connect me to them, and to others, seemed more important than such questions. Ever since that first moment of realization, I have felt deeply grateful for the way in which this piece of cloth serves as a bridge, inviting me to feel and express greater love for God, to receive comfort and hope from Mary, and to connect me with my Christian faith and with the faith of all those who have prayed near it for centuries.

Many of my Catholic friends who are wary of the superstition they link with relics find it hard to believe that I am so devoted to praying in the presence of Mary's Veil. Some tease me about encouraging pilgrims to spend time in silent reflection and connection with God while sitting near it. I understand; it surprises me too. But if God wants to use an American woman minister to introduce others to praying with a Catholic relic in France, who am I to say no? After all, Mary's strong example challenges me to say yes to God in the strangest of situations.

Throughout the course of my search for images, symbols, history, and liturgical traditions relating to Mary at Chartres, Jesus has been introducing me to his mother. My prayers in the morning by the veil, and in the evening at the ecumenical Vespers service, including the daily singing of Mary's Magnificat (Luke 1:46–55), have opened my heart to knowing Mary as more than a biblical character. I have found her deep in my heart, in a place that resonates when I study carefully the images I'm creating, sense my mother's love for my family, the church and the world, and when I kneel in silence contemplating the mystery that is God.

Quite unexpectedly, Mary has helped me to know her son better. While searching for Mary, I couldn't help noticing that at Chartres Cathedral, in centuries of worship as in imagery, Mary's roles as mother and disciple involve a willingness to direct attention to Christ. Her love for God empowered her to serve Jesus. While it is possible to look at images like the one at the right and see Mary, it is also possible to view it and focus on Jesus. My experience of Christ has been more than anything that of an older brother who was also God. The Marian imagery in the cathedral challenged me to open myself to knowing Christ more fully.

I am deeply grateful for all the time I have spent photographing and studying the hundreds of images and symbols of Mary from nine centuries of devotion at Chartres Cathedral. I have come to sense Mary's powerful role among the multitudes of the faithful through the ages, whose vision and work built the cathedral and whose devotion made and make it the pilgrimage church it is today. I hope you will come and experience the cathedral yourself—first in the pages of this book, and, if the doors open for you, in person.

MARY, OUR LADY
OF CHARTRES

I pray that you may have the power to comprehend, with all the saints,
what is the breadth and length and height and depth, and to know the
love of Christ that surpasses knowledge, so that you may be filled with
all the fullness of God. (Ephesians 3:18–19)

Mary, her love, and the love of others for her is the heart of the story of Chartres Cathedral. *Notre-Dame de Chartres*, Our Lady of Chartres, is an architectural marvel, a stunning showcase for the most complete twelfth- and thirteenth-century collection of stained glass in the world. Its history may have begun by the fourth century, although little documentation exists about its early years. During the seventh century, Bétaire, the bishop of Chartres, is said to have prayed at an altar for the Virgin at Chartres. In the following century, the building was named the Church of Mary, one of the first churches in the West to bear this name. Chartres became forever linked with Mary when Emperor Charles the Bald offered a relic associated with her to the cathedral in 876.

"Mary's Veil" is a piece of silk that she is said to have worn during the Annunciation and birth of Jesus. For over twelve centuries it has drawn millions of pilgrims to Chartres Cathedral. Its survival during a devastating fire of the town and cathedral in 1194 was considered miraculous, and taken as a sign that Mary desired a bigger, more beautiful church. To grant her this wish, an expensive and extensive building program began immediately. It was completed less than thirty

years later, around 1220. One need only look at the many windows or sculptures of this period to see how profound and pervasive was the devotion to Mary that inspired this cathedral.

The many engaging images of Mary and her son at Chartres Cathedral are difficult to appreciate with the naked eye. To make them more accessible, the photographs and prose in this book present the story of Mary at Chartres up close. Here, text and photos are placed side by side to invite both reflection and contemplation. Those who wish a broad understanding of the range of Marian images and themes at Chartres Cathedral will want to read this book from cover to cover. Others may choose to thumb through and find their favorite images and learn more about them. One need only turn the pages to appreciate the depth and breadth of devotion to Mary expressed in the images gathered over almost a millennium in the vast cathedral of Notre-Dame de Chartres, "Our Lady of Chartres."

There are many ways one could think about how Mary is portrayed in the cathedral. As I considered the best way to organize the many images of her, the theme of her motherhood, although obviously not all-inclusive, brought them together for me. Perhaps it was because my own relationship with my children is so vital to my life. Also, I so readily relate to her experiences as a mother—her contemplative nature as she parented, her surrender to be a mother when she could not possibly have been "ready," her belief in her son's mission, her relationship with Jesus that included honesty and respect, and her willingness to open her mother's heart to all of life, even suffering when the time for that came.

The motherhood theme made sense to me as a theologian as well. Although I didn't grow up with much exposure to Mary, I always thought of her as a strong woman. During my graduate work in women's studies, I came to appreciate that any role be can shaped and used by those who have power. While some contemporary women and men might devalue motherhood as limiting a woman's "potential," I find it fascinating, even exciting, to wonder about just how meaningful it is that God trusted Godself first to a woman's body, and then to a mother's loving nurture.

Hearing that the Church officially acknowledged that Mary is the Mother of God beginning in the fifth century can be unsettling. But when one understands that this does not mean that she was God before Jesus, but that God really did depend on a woman to become a human being, it is easier to embrace. It seems important for our modern eyes to consider what this looked like to our forebears in the Middle Ages. The images they created of Mary as the Mother of God tell us much about Christ. They also suggest a way to think about God's deep value of women.

On one extreme, some people see the images of Mary as the throne of Jesus that pepper the cathedral as devaluing a woman because she is used to put forth a man, and on the other extreme, some see her as a goddess with her small and less important child. What if Mary as the Throne of God's Wisdom (*Sedes Sapientiae*) is an expression of the essential nature of mutuality and balance—little and big, woman and man, human and God, to name a few.

As a woman minister, called by God and ordained by the American Baptist Churches since 1984, I have experienced the ways in which God has used my experiences of my mother and of being a mother to shape and inform my pastoral service. Obviously, I have also experienced resistance to my ministry, as one man told me, "because you are a woman and the Bible doesn't let women be ministers." I respect each person's and church's right to discern in faith through Scriptures, their own history, and traditions how women and men may serve. I also think it is important for all of us to allow our theology to be influenced by what those with the least access to power can help us to understand. For example, if a poor, young, single woman from the Middle East became the Mother of the Church, then what can she teach us? By taking a close look at the (primarily) medieval images of Mary as she came to be understood by Christ's church as its mother, we may gain new insight into God's perspective relating to women's

service in the contemporary church. It might invite us to see things we haven't yet considered.

When I look at the images of Mary at Chartres, where she is almost never portrayed alone, I see Jesus and then I see Mary, but I also see the people around them. Many biblical and nonbiblical images in the cathedral portray Mary and Jesus as they are found with those who need help, want to say thanks, are family members, disciples, donors, or witnesses. Devotion to Christ and to Mary call out to our own sense of wanting to be with them, and of wanting them to share in our lives.

Finally, any work on Mary at Chartres would be incomplete without expressing how in a global sense she serves as the mother of us all. One can identify the images that point to this role, but equally significant are the thousands of daily expressions of veneration of Mary that continue as pilgrims and church members pray in the cathedral.

The pages that follow depict and explore the depth and breadth of Marian imagery at Chartres, as seen through four lenses of her motherhood. Portrayals of Mary as Mother of Jesus, Mother of God, Mother of the Church, and Mother of us all will beckon readers to open more widely their hearts, minds, and theologies, so that ultimately they may know, love, and serve God in fresh and more beautiful ways.

Chapter One

MARY,
MOTHER OF JESUS

1.1 INTRODUCTION

*Now the birth of Jesus the Messiah took place in this way.
When his mother Mary had been engaged to Joseph,
but before they lived together, she was found to be
with child from the Holy Spirit.*

—MATTHEW 1:18

J esus's humanity depended on Mary's maternity. Just as every human being's life relies on their mother's, so too Jesus developed in Mary's womb. He was born amid her labor, was nourished by the food she provided, and grew up under her care and oversight.

As Jesus's mother, Mary was given a unique role in God's plan of salvation. Only one of the biblical stories about Mary does not specifically focus on her relationship with her earthly son. (For this exception, see Acts 1:13–14, where Mary is mentioned as praying with the disciples after Jesus's death—see p. 60). Each of the biblical stories that sheds light on Mary as Jesus's mother as he was conceived, was born, and grew up is portrayed in the cathedral, often many times. These include the annunciation of Jesus's conception and birth (Luke 1:26–38); the visitation of Mary and her kinswoman Elizabeth (Luke 1:39–56); Mary's place in the genealogy of Jesus (Matthew 1:16); the story of Joseph's visit from an angel telling him to take Mary as his wife and Jesus's subsequent birth (Matthew 1:18–25); Mary's delivery of Jesus followed by the shepherd's visit to the Holy Family (Luke 2:1–20); Mary and Joseph's fulfillment of the parental responsibility of presenting Jesus in the temple (Luke 2:22–39); the visit of the Magi to Jesus and his mother (Matthew 2:11); the Holy Family's flight to Egypt (Matthew 2:13–15—see detail on left); their return from Egypt (Matthew 2:19–21); Mary and Joseph's search for Jesus in Jerusalem after the Passover when Jesus was twelve (Luke 2:41–51); Mary and Jesus's talk at the wedding in Cana (John 2:1–12); and Mary's presence as Jesus was being crucified (John 19:25–27).

The entries in this chapter introduce images that relate to these biblical stories, illustrating the varied ways artists and theologians from the twelfth and thirteenth centuries at Chartres imagined Mary as the mother of Jesus.

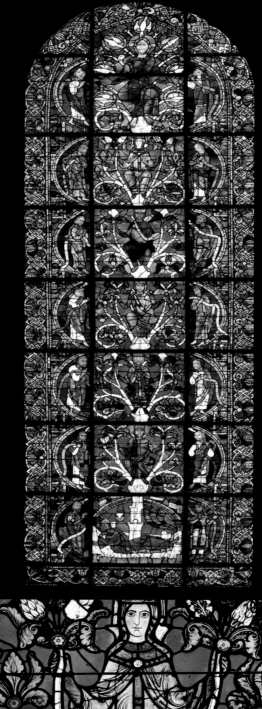

1.2 MARY, DESCENDANT OF KING DAVID

A shoot shall come out from the stump of Jesse,
and a branch shall grow out of his roots. (Isaiah 11:1–2)

At the bottom of this stained-glass window Jesse (left), the father of the Old Testament king David, sleeps. From his reclining body, a tree with royal and prophetic progeny grows. In the center of its trunk and branches are four seated kings from the Old Testament. Mary sits above them and below Jesus, a visual reminder of both scriptural and apocryphal references to her Davidic lineage cited by the church fathers. In biblical times, it was customary to marry within one's own tribe (see Matthew 1:1–16 for Joseph's lineage); it was assumed by early writers that Mary and Joseph followed this practice. Mary's placement in the window shows her as the woman who linked the Hebrew and Christian people of God, and more expansively, earth and heaven.

Mary's relationship to the Old Testament prophetic tradition is here made evident. The Chartres image, unlike many earlier manuscript versions of the Tree of Jesse, includes two rows of seven Major and Minor Prophets who foretold the coming of the Messiah and the virgin birth. They stand on either side of the window. Their names appear on the scrolls they hold.

The Tree of Jesse imagery appeared prominently in the eleventh century. It sprang from centuries of Old Testament readings in worship, especially the liturgy of the Feast of Mary's Nativity, which Bishop Fulbert had introduced at Chartres in the eleventh century. The link between Jesse and Jesus was also one of the themes addressed in medieval liturgical dramas that would have taken place in the cathedral. Stained-glass images, like this twelfth-century window at Chartres, help us to understand more about how biblical images served theological purposes. For instance, Mary's size and position help the viewer to see that while privileged to be near her son—at the feet of the Son of God, as it were—she is present both to fulfill and to reveal God's purpose in history.

1.3 MARY, DAUGHTER OF ANNE

Jesus's grandmother is depicted several times at Chartres. Mary's care and love for her son, Jesus, are foreshadowed in the images of Anne with her daughter Mary.

A young Mary rests in the arms of her mother, Anne, in the central lancet window under the North Rose at Chartres Cathedral. They both have golden halos, indicating their holiness. Anne holds a scepter with three flowers, which likely symbolizes the rod of King David's father, Jesse (Isaiah 11:1), and foreshadows Jesus's place in that royal lineage. Mary leans back on her mother's shoulder, illustrating the steady support that her mother provided. Mary is clothed in white and holds a book in both hands. This symbolic depiction of Mary's holding the Word of God appears throughout the cathedral.

Mary's parents never appear in the New Testament, but they do in the *Proto-evangelium of James*, an apocryphal book that was well-known at Chartres in the Middle Ages. In the cathedral, extrabiblical images of Mary based on this work, including depictions of her mother, Anne, and her father, Joachim, emphasize Mary's heritage as a descendant of the tribe of David (see p. 12), her miraculous birth to infertile parents, and the unique spiritual formation of Mary at the temple in Jerusalem, which prepared her to be Jesus's mother.

Many relics were transported to Europe after 1204, when the Byzantine capital of Constantinople was sacked by Western crusaders. Among these was the purported skull of Mary's mother, Anne. The widow of Count Louis of Blois-Chartres offered it to the cathedral when it arrived in Chartres. The presence of this relic influenced the inclusion of sculpture and stained-glass images of Anne. It influenced the liturgy as well. Anne's skull later disappeared, perhaps during the French Revolution.

1.4 MARY AND THE WORD OF GOD

Chartres was a renowned medieval center of learning for those preparing for clerical life. The School of Chartres reached the height of its influence in the eleventh and twelfth centuries, when prominent theologians such as Gilbert of Poitiers, William of Conches, Thierry of Chartres, and John of Salisbury taught at this institution. The students' core curriculum revolved around the seven liberal arts: logic, grammar, and rhetoric (the Trivium), as well as arithmetic, geometry, music, and astronomy (the Quadrivium).

Teachings from the School of Chartres appear visually in the windows and sculptures at the cathedral. In the thirteenth-century Life of Mary window, the academic context itself is highlighted.

Although the Bible is silent about any formal education on Mary's part, apocryphal gospels speak of Mary's training between the ages of three and fourteen in the temple of Jerusalem. This image strays from that tradition, placing her in a schoolroom and among boys. Only Mary's head with its long hair is encircled by a halo, emphasizing her sanctity. She carefully studies a book on her lap. While Mary's classmates are interacting with their teacher, Mary's attention is more internally focused, recalling Luke's description of her as one who pondered the meaning of her experiences (Luke 1:29; 2:19).

The coupling of Mary and a book may seem odd to modern viewers who are accustomed to thinking of Jesus's mother as a poor, uneducated girl. Medieval artists, seeking ways to symbolize Mary's carrying of the Word of God in her womb as Jesus, often showed her carrying a book.

1.5 DIRECTING OTHERS TO JESUS

The first window one sees when walking into Chartres Cathedral from the main door in the west is directly ahead near the choir vault at the far end of the church. If one looks carefully, it is possible to identify Gabriel and Mary. Although they are hard to see from so far away without binoculars, the image portrays them as they exchange an intense, knowing look. As close as they are to each other, they are separated by a red column, reminding the viewer that they live in two different domains.

Above Mary's head, a haloed dove, the same color as Gabriel's heavenly blue wings, descends. It is entering Mary's halo, signifying the conception of Jesus within Mary's body.

Gabriel and Mary's hands demonstrate one of the deeper levels of meaning in this image of the annunciation of Jesus's conception (Luke 1:26–38). Gabriel wraps his left hand around a staff topped with a golden fleur-de-lis. As a bare-footed angelic messenger of God (Isaiah 52:7), he has come to make a proclamation on behalf of the King. He raises his right pointer finger both symbolizing his oratory role and directing attention to Mary, God's chosen vessel.

Mary, pressing a book against her womb with her left hand, another symbolic reference to her divine pregnancy, embodies the message that the Word and her body are being united. Mary's right hand is gently turned upward as if she were cupping her heart. Her first finger points toward a part of the neighboring window where God, depicted with the face and nimbus of Christ, is shown appearing to Moses in the midst of a flaming bush. As is the norm at Chartres Cathedral, although Mary's special role is highlighted, she directs attention toward God.

1.6 FROM HER WOMB: A KING IS BORN

The colors of this nativity image, near its bottom, show the theological significance of God's coming into the world as Jesus.

The blue that covers Mary's and Jesus's bodies and surrounds their heads reminds the viewer of the sky. The heavenly nature of Mary's pregnancy and Christ's divinity comes into focus. The white of Mary's Veil, upper garment, and pillow signify her virginal purity. It is mirrored in the open curtains, their cloudlike white set between bands of sky blue; the heavens have been opened to reveal God incarnate.

Green carries the message of life. It surrounds Mary, who has carried Life in her womb, and is shown lining the manger where Jesus lies. At Chartres, this same green is seen in stained-glass images of Jesus's crucifixion (see p. 57), for even in death Christ brought life to the world. As John says, "In him was life, and the life was the light of all people" (1:4).

The blood red that forms the background of the stained-glass image signifies that Jesus, was the One "whom God put forward as a sacrifice of atonement by his blood" (Romans 3:25).

Gold was considered the color of divine light. The golden star in the upper right-hand corner foretells the arrival of the Wise Men from the East who observed the king's star rising (Matthew 2:1–2). But before their arrival, the donkey and ox already bear witness to this miracle, a theme first voiced by the prophet Isaiah (1:3) and later enshrined in the apocryphal Gospel of Pseudo-Matthew and rendered in the great thirteenth-century hymn *O Magnum Mysterium* (O Great Mystery).

This baby, portrayed not in a traditional manger but raised up on a golden altarlike platform supported by golden columns, will later be sacrificed both on the cross and subsequently on the altars of the church. Above him, a flame burns that resembled that which would have been found by the tabernacle, where the consecrated hosts, the presence of God in the Eucharist, would have been and still are reserved for veneration.

1.7 PONDERING THE MYSTERY

Mary gazes in the direction of her newborn son while resting her face on the fingers of her right hand (left). At the same time, she gently pulls back the cloth wrapped around Jesus's neck with her left hand. The tender, pensive look on Mary's face is unusual in sculptural depictions of Jesus's birth carved in the thirteenth century.

Although Mary touches both her body and Jesus's, her attention seems far away; she seems lost in thought or deep in prayer. Her eyes, which still show remnants of the original paint, are open. When Mary was alive, it was still common to pray with open eyes. Her mouth is closed and her ears are covered. This image seems to fit with the two biblical references that speak of Mary pondering what was happening (Luke 1:26–29 and 2:16–19).

These sculptures were placed at least sixteen feet above parishioners in a niche of the rood screen that separated the nave from the choir. They were a part of a series of seven scenes that depicted different reactions to the Christ child by his mother, the shepherds, Herod, the Magi, and those in the temple when Joseph and Mary brought him there for the first time.

Mary lies on a bed and leans toward her son. She gently reveals him with her fingers. This image, placed in an area dedicated to the prayers of the laypeople at the end of the nave, mirrors what was happening on the other side of the rood screen. There, in the choir, the exclusive domain of the medieval clergy, priests both touched and revealed the body of Christ as they celebrated each Mass.

The rood screen was dismantled in 1763. Many of the sculptural fragments were placed facedown and used to repair the cathedral floor. Most were rediscovered in 1848–49. While they are currently in storage, there are plans to display them permanently in the cathedral's Piat Chapel when its restoration is complete.

1.8 OFFERING HER SON TO GOD

Jesus, shown as a young boy, is the visual focus of the Presentation in the Temple image from the twelfth century (right). A square altar that represents both Jesus's required redemption as a firstborn Jewish son (Exodus 13:1–2, 14–15, Luke 2:22–23) and his sacrificial death, which would bring God's salvation (Luke 2:25–32) is also in the center. The way Mary and Simeon, a righteous and devout man from Jerusalem who was waiting for the consolation of Israel (Luke 2:25), raise Jesus above the altar foreshadows the lifting of the Host at each Eucharist, a liturgical practice added to the Mass around the time this image was created.

Mary was required to come to the temple for ritual purification forty days after her son's birth (Leviticus 12:6–7). She brought Jesus to present him to the Lord at the same time. Mary stands on the left side of this image, her head encircled by an immense blue halo. She is represented as a faithful Jewish mother, fulfilling all the Mosaic laws as they applied to her family. Her gaze directs the viewer to her son.

Simeon stands facing Mary on the right. He looks to Jesus as he receives him from his mother. Simeon praises God and prophesies over Jesus, calling him "a light for revelation to the Gentiles" (Luke 2:32). Jesus's yellow outer garment and halo, as well as Mary's garment that falls from the area of her womb, symbolize this light.

The Feasts of Mary's Purification and the Presentation of Jesus were celebrated each year on February 2. This feast day also came to be known as Candlemas, the day on which all the candles to be used in the coming year were dedicated. In the Middle Ages, the congregation at Chartres celebrated these feasts, processing with lighted candles. They would circle the inside of the cathedral, and then move outside, where below another sculpted image of Jesus's presentation on the south tympanum of the west wall they sang of God's revelation in Christ, the light of the world (John 8:12). Image and liturgy were used together to reveal the fullness of the theological truths they embodied.

1.9 SAFELY IN HER ARMS

The Holy Family's flight to Egypt, as depicted in this early thirteenth-century window, shows the importance of Mary and Joseph's parental role of protecting their son. Joseph, who has been warned to flee to Egypt in a dream (Matthew 2:13–15), carries a pilgrim's staff as he leads the donkey while looking over his left shoulder.

Mary sits sideways on a donkey. Although there is no animal in the biblical account, it is referenced twice in the apocryphal gospel referred to as *Pseudo-Matthew* (chapters 17 and 20), which clearly influenced this and the other six depictions of this story at Chartres. Mary cradles a swaddled Jesus with her right arm and hand. She secures him next to her body with her left hand. The infant Jesus's halo bears the mark of the cross, a commonplace practice in medieval art meant to remind us that from the time of his birth we witness a presentiment of his death.

From the top of the image, the hand of God is shown pointing toward Jesus, whose body is aligned with this gesture, in the act of blessing. This celestial hand is found in many windows at Chartres, often in scenes that depict the holy protagonists in difficulty or facing martyrdom. Here, it is striking, too, that Jesus is surrounded by three caring hands, Mary's two hands and the "hand" of the Father.

The underlying theme of this image is security. Joseph is shown protecting Mary and Jesus, moving them forward to Egypt as he tugs on the donkey's lead but with his eyes also focused on the vulnerable infant and his mother. Mary's secure embrace of her son, tender and firm, is a position often used by mothers for protection and comfort. Beyond simply holding Jesus, Mary fixes her eyes on his as he looks directly back. Their gaze is steady and supported by their red halos, which seem to create a cocoon around them. God's protective hand "watches over them" from on high.

1.10 A MOTHER'S INFLUENCE

In this image, Jesus and Mary stand near each other. Jesus's outer garment touches Mary's cloak; one senses both the distance and closeness between them. Mary looks toward Jesus's face as if trying to see what he is going to do, while Jesus gazes beyond her into the distance as if looking toward the future. Jesus, taller than his mother, blesses her with his right hand; both carry a book in their left hands, while Mary, wearing a veil, holds her right hand in front of her with her palm open, a gesture of acceptance that appears in many Annunciation images. Jesus's right foot extends beyond the framed boundary, suggesting action, while Mary's covered feet seem static.

Six thirteenth-century scenes near the bottom of the Blue Virgin Window depict the biblical story of the wedding at Cana, which includes Jesus's first miracle (John 2:1–11). The third image (left) illustrates Jesus's willingness to listen to his mother and follow her promptings. Its message is foundational to the Catholic and Orthodox theological understanding of Mary's role as Mediatrix, a title used for Mary since at least the fifth century to describe her intercessory role.

This image illustrates a key interchange that occurred during the wedding:

> There was a wedding in Cana of Galilee, and the mother of Jesus was there. Jesus and his disciples had also been invited to the wedding. When the wine gave out, the mother of Jesus said to him, "They have no wine." And Jesus said to her, "Woman, what concern is that to you and to me? My hour has not yet come." (John 2:1–4)

Although Jesus resisted his mother's request at first, in the end he did as she asked, turning water into wine (vv. 5–11). This story, as well as this image, has encouraged many over the centuries who have prayed to Mary, asking for help in presenting their needs to God.

—✦—

## Chapter Two

MARY,
MOTHER OF GOD

2.1 INTRODUCTION

*[King Solomon] also made a great ivory throne,
and overlaid it with the finest gold. The throne had six steps.
The top of the throne was rounded in the back, and on each
side of the seat were arm rests and two lions standing beside
the arm rests, while twelve lions were standing,
one on each end of a step on the six steps.
Nothing like it was ever made in any kingdom.*

—1 KINGS 10:18–20 [repeated in 2 Chronicles 9:17–19]

Italian Cardinal Peter Damian (d. 1073) was the first to compare Mary to Solomon's throne. As the great King Solomon dispensed wisdom from his magnificent throne, so the Wisdom of God incarnate (Christ Jesus) sits on the lap of Mary, his mother. The Throne of Wisdom image of Mary and Jesus was placed extensively throughout the cathedral of Chartres. A crowned Mary, often with her veil flowing over her head and shoulders, sits on a throne supporting Jesus with one hand, and lifts a scepter, symbolizing royal power, with the other. Jesus sits squarely on her lap looking forward, normally holding a closed book. His other hand, with its palm facing the viewer, blesses with his two extended first fingers.

Many questions come to mind among contemporary Protestants and others who are not familiar with religious symbolism when they look at this type of depiction of Mary as the Mother of God. "Does the fact that Mary is shown as 'bigger' than Jesus mean that she is being depicted as more important?" "Why does this young Jesus have the face of an adult man?" "Why is Mary, who was probably a peasant girl in her teens when Jesus was born, shown as a mature woman with the symbols of royalty?" "If Mary is shown as a queen, why doesn't Jesus, the true King of Kings (Revelation 19:16), have a crown or other signs of his regal role?"

After learning that this type of image is called "Mary, the Throne of Wisdom" (Sedes Sapientiae), more questions follow: "Is Mary sitting on a throne or is she acting like a throne for Jesus?" "Where in the Bible do these images come from?" and, "What do they signify?"

The entries of this chapter shed light on these questions, explaining why the Throne of Wisdom image is so important at Chartres and how it helps one to understand what it means that Mary is the Mother of God.

2.2 MARY, THE GOD-BEARER

Mary was officially declared to be Theotokos, or God-bearer, in 431 at a council held in Ephesus (in present-day Turkey). In the early church, prominent bishops and theologians had disagreed about the nature of Jesus. At this ecumenical council, the gathered bishops affirmed that he was both human and divine. Their declaration had implications for who they understood Mary to be as well.

Created by the French sculptor Charles-Antoine Bridan in 1788, this bas-relief depicts the meeting in Ephesus. Eleven of the council members, seen sitting in a large semicircle, discuss Jesus's nature. The dove placed at the top and in the center, representing the Holy Spirit, sends forth rays of wisdom as the council members agree that Jesus was both God and human. Cyril, patriarch of Alexandria (Egypt), sitting high in the presider's seat, is delivering a judgment against Nestorius, the patriarch of Constantinople (now Istanbul, Turkey), shown in the foreground on the floor. The iconography is reminiscent of images of the Last Supper with Judas often turning away or separated from the other disciples.

Nestorius believed that while Christ had both divine and human natures, they were separate, such that while Jesus's humanity was born of Mary, his divinity was born of God. Hence, he spoke of Mary as *Christotokos*, or "Christ-bearer." Cyril and the council opposed this name, insisting that the two natures could not be separated. Nestorius's cowering posture, the broken bishop's staff that is still in his hand, and the two lightning bolts that point toward him from the stormy sky all illustrate that his christological views had been deemed heretical.

Accepting Jesus's mysterious dual nature allowed the council to declare Mary *Theotokos*. This Greek word is often translated into English as Mother of God or God-bearer. (*Birth-giver of God* is a more literal rendering). The importance of these terms is that they point out the presence of God in the Incarnation.

This bas relief in the choir is one of a series of eight sculpted scenes (two are now in the local museum).

2.3 MARY, THE THRONE FOR GOD'S WISDOM

The Virgin and Child in Majesty seated above the south door greet all who approach Chartres Cathedral from the west. This is the earliest depiction of its type at the cathedral, having been sculpted around 1145. The statues from this tympanum are severely damaged, yet the large central sculptural group, especially Mary and Jesus, still communicates much of its original message.

Both mother and son face forward and gaze directly ahead. Haloes encircle their heads; Jesus's nimbus has its traditional three-armed-cross uniquely reserved for him. The incensing angels on each side suggest the sacred importance of both Jesus and his mother.

Mary sits regally as the Queen Mother. Her large crown, decorated throne, and footstool all emphasize her royalty. Her right hand protectively holds her young son. Mary's Veil, so precious at Chartres, is visible on the sides of her head.

Jesus sits squarely on Mary's lap. He has a child's body and the face of a man, as is often the case in medieval depictions. This image was used to insist on the coexistence of his incarnated humanity as well as his eternal divinity.

Jesus's hands are missing. At Notre-Dame de Paris, in a remarkably similar sculpture, Jesus's arms are in identical positions: with his left hand he holds a book representing, among other things, the wisdom of God, with his right hand, he performs the priestly action of blessing.

This type of image is often referred to as *Sedes Sapientiae*, a Latin devotional title for Mary meaning the "seat" or "throne" of divine wisdom. Mary was understood to be the New Testament equivalent of the throne of Solomon described in 1 Kings 10:18–20. The Old Testament royal line of King David has flowed through Mary to her son.

Jesus sits on Mary's lap, showing that his humanity depends on her. Mary supports her child, who embodies the Wisdom of God.

2.5 THE FULFILLMENT OF ALL
THAT HAS COME BEFORE

But when the fullness of time had come, God sent his Son, born of a
woman, born under the law. (Galatians 4:4)

Mary sits in the center of the kaleidoscopelike North Rose Window,
holding Jesus as he rests against her. She is clothed in an earthy brown
garment, celestial blue cape, and pure white veil that covers her head
and drapes down into her lap, as if disappearing under her son. Jesus
wears a golden robe symbolizing divine light and wisdom, and a green
outer garment, representing life. Mary's unusually large blue halo
resembles the nimbus that circles her head in the Blue Virgin Window
(see p. 50). Jesus's cruciform halo is blood red with a white cross.

Symbols that relate to their royal heritage in the family of David
surround Jesus and Mary. The twelve kings of Judah, the tribe to which
Jesus belonged, sit inside twelve offset squares. Like Mary, they are all
crowned and hold royal scepters. The twelve Minor Prophets of the
Old Testament, known for proclaiming the future coming of Christ,
stand as sentinels in the twelve outer circles.

The north side of cathedrals, being the coldest and darkest, were
decorated with images that related to Old Testament times. The natural
way one would "read" divine history upon entering a medieval church
from the west would be to move to the left (north) and proceed around
the church toward the right (south).

This thirty-four-foot wall of glass (right) that was donated by Queen
Blanche of Castile, regent of France from 1226–1234, tells the biblical
message of God's fulfillment of the Old Testament prophecies about
the coming of Christ. Mary is shown as the bridge between the Old
Testament and the New.

The incarnation of God in Jesus is the center of all that has come
before.

2.6 MARY'S SUPPORT

Through Jesus's presence in his mother's body, God ushered in a new era. For this reason, Mary has long been considered the link between Old and New Testament times. It is not surprising, then, to find her standing and holding Jesus in the central lancet under the South Rose Window, where prophets and Gospel writers flank them. The four Old Testament prophets, identified by their names written underneath them, are Jeremiah, Isaiah, Ezekiel, and Daniel; the four New Testament Evangelists, also identified by name, are sitting on the prophets' shoulders. They are, from left to right, Luke, Matthew, John, and Mark.

These thirteenth-century windows visually interpret a twelfth-century teaching from the School of Chartres. John of Salisbury, bishop of Chartres until 1176, wrote in the *Metalogicon*, "Bernard of Chartres used to say that we [the moderns] are like dwarves perched on the shoulders of giants [the ancients], and thus we are able to see more and farther than the latter. And this is not at all because of the acuteness of our sight or the stature of our body, but because we are carried aloft and elevated by the magnitude of the giants."

Both Old Testament prophets and the New Testament Evangelists had importance for the church, although the Gospel writers recorded a fuller understanding of God. Mary and Jesus were both valued by the church, but Jesus was God, while Mary was the one who bore God. In the central lancet, we see Jesus, dwarfed in size, but not in power. This young human boy with the now familiar face of an adult man, symbolizing his divinity, blesses all who look to him.

In images that depict Mary as Jesus's mother during his infancy, it is not her large size that is significant. It is her support of Jesus. Here, he doesn't sit on her lap, she holds him up, and he sees farther than anyone has ever seen—all the way to God's eternal purposes.

2.7 OUR LADY OF THE CRYPT

Our Lady of the Crypt, cherished through the centuries by pilgrims and parishioners at Chartres Cathedral, has been represented by different wooden statues that have closely resembled one another. The current version, shown in color, is a walnut statue carved in 1976. This *Notre-Dame de Sous-Terre* statue replaced a cedar version offered in 1857 that was later kept at the Carmel Monastery in Chartres (small image at left). This nineteenth-century version was a near replica of the older Black Virgin and Child, whose initial historical reference appeared in 1389. In 1791, after the crypt was closed during the French Revolution, the statue was moved to the upper church and in 1793 was taken outside the cathedral and burned. A popular legend, first recorded in the second quarter of the sixteenth century, speaks of an even more ancient statue of a virgin who would give birth that had been worshiped in a grotto on the site of the current cathedral.

The Old Testament prophecy of Isaiah "Behold, a virgin shall conceive, and bear a son" (7:14 KJV) was understood as a reference to Mary and Jesus. It was often referenced in the medieval stained glass, sculptures, and worship at Chartres. The Virgin who is about to give birth (*virgini pariturae*) was celebrated in the liturgy at Chartres for at least two centuries before the creation of the medieval statue of the Virgin Mother.

Notre-Dame de Sous-Terre serves, as earlier statues did for centuries, as a focal point of prayer for those who descend to the crypt. Mary, crowned and serving as a throne for her son, supports him as he sits on her lap. Mary's closed eyes suggest her contemplative nature, as well as her limited understanding of all that was to come. Jesus, with open eyes, looks knowingly to the future. One of the powerful possibilities of these images is the way they invite viewers to see Mary and Jesus as interconnected, and yet as each having a different place in God's plan for humanity.

2.8 ROYALTY MEETS ROYALTY

Matthew describes the visit of Magi (2:1–2), the priests and philosophers from the East, to Jesus, the king of the Jews and his mother.

> On entering the house, they saw the child with Mary his mother; and they knelt down and paid him homage. Then, opening their treasure chests, they offered him gifts of gold, frankincense, and myrrh. (2:11)

This twelfth-century image of the Wise Men's visit in the Infancy of Christ Window on the west wall strays from the biblical text. Instead, it depicts a medieval theological commentary of the Epiphany story. The Wise Men of Scripture have become crowned kings. These regal visitors signify the recognition of the kingship of Jesus by Gentiles, and fulfill the prophecies about the kings in Psalm 72:10–11 and of Isaiah 60:3.

The crowned Queen Mother, Mary, sits on a richly decorated throne that places her higher than the visiting kings. Her oversized hand (signifying her special connection with the divine) holds a flowering scepter representing her sovereignty and the kingship of her son. The liturgy during the Feast of the Epiphany, represented by this image, celebrated the royal heritage of Jesus and Mary. The genealogy of Jesus from Luke (3:23–28), with its emphasis on the kingly lineage of the house of David, was the Gospel reading during the morning service of Matins each Epiphany.

In this image Jesus holds a book, symbolizing the wisdom that is available to him as well as the "Word" of Scripture, which points to him. His right hand is disproportionately large as if to emphasize his divinity and superior power as he blesses the three arriving kings. His extended fingers also point to the star in the pane of glass to the left that has led the Wise Men (Matthew 2:2, 9) to him. Although Jesus's size signals his infant status as he sits on Mary's lap, he is already functioning as God's wise, chosen ruler.

2.9 OUR LADY OF THE PILLAR

Notre-Dame du Pilier is a sculpture of a young Mary holding a pear with one hand and a bare-footed Jesus with the other. Her son sits securely on her left knee, blessing with his right hand and holding a globelike ball with his other.

This sculpture has held a special place in the hearts of both laypeople and clergy for five centuries. There is still a steady stream of parishioners, visitors, and pilgrim groups flowing in and out of the Pillar Chapel all day long. Placed on a pillar from the thirteenth-century choir rood screen, this sixteenth-century statue of Mary and her son holds the attention of those who sit on well-worn prayer benches, or kneel on cushions. Votive candles flicker nearby, representing the deepest needs and longings of human hearts. Their glow just outside the chapel adds warmth and softness to the prayer-soaked environment.

Our Lady of the Pillar, sculpted from pear wood in 1508, is a copy of a much revered thirteenth-century statue. Originally it sat atop a pillar of the rood screen that separated the nave, where laypeople were free to move, from the choir, where only the clergy, who were conducting services, were allowed. Thus people could come and pray near the statue without interrupting the liturgies taking place on the other side of the thick stone screen. Already within a century of its introduction, a local historian named Sebastian Rouillard wrote that kisses had worn away the stone pillar on which the sculpture rested. The tradition of concluding one's prayer by kissing the pillar continues to this day.

The statue was restored in 2013. The removal of the remnants of a layer of black paint applied by clergy during the early twentieth century, and the addition of a lighter one to areas of Mary and Jesus's skin shocked many who had come to consider the sculpture a black Virgin. As the cathedral and its sacred objects undergo restoration, changes, both welcome and unwanted, are integrated into the ongoing story of faith and practice.

2.10 BELOVED MOTHER AND CHILD

The Blue Virgin Window, as this stained-glass image is known in English, speaks first with color. Mary's blue halo and outer garment engage and amaze the viewer as only the blue glass of Chartres from the twelfth century can. The red background, recalling Christ's blood, as well as symbolizing the love of God, creates a sense of expectancy.

Mary sits on a throne facing the viewer directly, serving as a throne for her son, who also faces forward. Jesus's mature face reminds viewers that while truly human, he is also the eternal Son of God. An off-white fabric covers Mary's head and falls from her shoulders, a visual reminder of the Veil of Mary. Her crown is like the imperial crown of Charles the Bald (823–877), who donated the veil to Chartres. This crown was a part of the cathedral's treasury until the fourteenth century.

Mary's size indicates her importance, yet more significant is her mandorla or almond-like shape. Mandorlas were used in sacred art to indicate a significant passage. Jesus, surrounded by Mary's almondlike shape, holds a tablet with the Latin words of Luke 3:5 quoted from Isaiah 40:4, a prophetic reference used in the Advent liturgy to highlight God's acting in history on behalf of those in need.

The censors swinging in the top of the image indicate the holiness of both Mary and Jesus. Their presence is an example of how images in medieval windows were in dialogue with the liturgies practiced nearby, and how liturgical acts could help to reveal the windows' theological meanings.

Jesus blesses with three fingers. Mary's right hand cups Jesus's shoulder protectively, while her other hand rests behind him, communicating support. While Mary is honored and venerated throughout the cathedral, this early image of her as the *Sedes Sapientiae* reminds viewers that although she had a unique place in divine history, her role as the Mother of God always involved revealing her son, who was also the Son of God.

Chapter Three

MARY, MOTHER OF THE CHURCH

3.1 INTRODUCTION

Just as the body is one and has many members,
and all the members of the body, though many,
are one body, so it is with Christ. . . .
Now you are the body of Christ and
individually members of it.

—1 CORINTHIANS 12:12, 27

3.2 JESUS'S COMMISSIONING OF MARY

The crucifixion of Jesus, with Mary on his right and John on his left, is the central theme of this thirteenth-century image at Chartres. The intensity and meaning of his death on the cross shine forth as well. The man with a sponge of wine or vinegar on the right (John 19:29) emphasizes Jesus's extreme suffering. The two attentive, haloed angels, one shown as male, the other shown as female, witnessing the scene from above remind viewers that God is not absent. The man piercing Jesus's side with a spear on the left (John 19:34) and Jesus's closed eyes signify that he is no longer alive. Rising from their graves, the two men at the bottom of the image suggest the future resurrection.

There is another important feature of this small rose window, located in the south ambulatory. Usually, Mary and John are shown well below the cross. Here, their feet are not visible; they emerge from undulating swaths of color that generally represent clouds. Their bodies are raised almost to the level of Jesus's outstretched arms. One of his nail-pierced hands extends into each of the two side-circles dedicated to Mary and John. Jesus's cross enters the space of their red haloes, visually connecting his mother and his disciple. This image illustrates the account in John's Gospel: "When Jesus saw his mother and the disciple whom he loved standing beside her [near the cross], he said to his mother, 'Woman, here is your son.' Then he said to the disciple, 'Here is your mother.' And from that hour the disciple took her into his own home" (John 19:26–27).

The church has traditionally understood these verses to mean that Jesus was giving Mary not only to John but to all who follow him. Mary's role as Jesus's mother is thus taking on new meaning as he dies and becomes the head of the church, for just as Mary was Jesus's earthly mother, she has now become the mother of his spiritual body, the church.

3.3 MARY AT THE EMPTY TOMB

The twelfth-century scene at Jesus's empty tomb (Mark 16:1–5) depicts familiar characters: a large winged angel wearing a white outer garment (left), three women stand holding containers of spices to anoint Jesus (center to right), and two soldiers who have fainted (bottom center and right, Matthew 28:4).

The sarcophagus is empty except for white linen wrappings (John 20:5–6). The two women in the front hold their left palms open in a gesture of greeting and acceptance. They look toward the angel, who is pointing to where Jesus's dead body had been. This is an illustration of the Gospel words "But [the angel] said to [the women], 'Do not be alarmed; you are looking for Jesus of Nazareth, who was crucified. He has been raised; he is not here. Look, there is the place they laid him. But go, tell his disciples and Peter that he is going ahead of you to Galilee; there you will see him, just as he told you'" (Mark 16:6–7).

The woman in the front has a small cross in the center of her white veil. Only Mary the mother of Jesus wears this iconic symbol above her forehead in medieval images. Scripture is silent about Jesus's mother's presence at the tomb after his resurrection. "Now it was Mary Magdalene, Joanna, Mary the mother of James, and the other women with them who told [what had happened at the tomb] to the apostles" could include her, although Church tradition never highlighted this (Luke 24:10). However, given the devotion to Mary at Chartres in the twelfth century, it is not completely surprising to find her represented in this scene.

Mary's placement closest to the angel, and presumably as the first to arrive at the tomb (in contrast to the sequence John tells in his Gospel), emphasizes her privileged position. This image also reflects the medieval emphasis on Mary's significant role in the early church. Even if the Bible did not mention her by name, Mary was honored as one of the post-Resurrection messengers who received and spread the news of her son's resurrection.

3.4 MARY'S EFFICACIOUS PRAYERS

Mary is the central figure in a group that includes eight praying apostles. Her large, praying hands rest at heart level. A veil covers her head and flows past her shoulders. On her lap a book lies wide open, for this is a post-Easter scene, and God's plan for the world had already been revealed in Christ's life, death, and resurrection.

This sculpture grouping was created in 1516 by an anonymous artist for the outer choir. It is the thirty-fifth in a sequence of forty scenes visible above the ambulatory that circles the choir. Although some interpreters refer to it as "Pentecost," close inspection shows that these sculptures instead depict the time after Jesus's ascension to heaven, yet before the coming of the Holy Spirit. The French inscription under the scene describes Mary's prayer, "Come Holy Spirit, descend on the apostles."

The sculptures to the left of this scene (see p. 55) show Jesus ascending to heaven. Just before he did this he told his disciples, "You will receive power when the Holy Spirit has come upon you; and you will be my witnesses in Jerusalem, in all Judea and Samaria, and to the ends of the earth" (Acts 1:8). Here, we see them praying, "for all the [apostles] were constantly devoting themselves to prayer, together with certain women, including Mary the mother of Jesus, as well as his brothers" (Acts 1:14).

This scene expresses the great faith believers have placed in the efficacy of Mary's prayer. As the central figure in this grouping, she is shown as the prime catalyst for Pentecost, when the Holy Spirit fell upon and animated the early disciples. In contrast to the others, most with their eyes open and lifted heavenward as if looking for the descent of the Spirit, Mary models a patient and inward attentiveness. While this image of her as Mediatrix is generally unknown to Protestants, its presence in such iconographic portrayals is self-evident to Catholics. These statues invite their viewers to have confidence in asking Mary to pray for the needs of the church, as well as for their personal needs.

3.5 SURROUNDED BY LOVE AT HER DEATH

Mary, shown with a red halo, lies on a bed in the foreground. Her head is propped up; she has closed her eyes. She is dying. Her uncharacteristic blue veil may foreshadow her transition to the heavenly realm.

Twelve haloed men, the apostles, gather near her bed. With grief written on all their faces, several also wipe tears from their eyes with their robes. In apocryphal accounts of Mary's death, the apostles converse and pray with Mary while she is dying, but this image emphasizes the emotional impact of her death on these men.

Mary's death and assumption into heaven are the central themes shown in the thirteenth-century Glorification of the Virgin Window. Two sources seem to stand behind this image, the fourth-century apocryphal document *The Book of John Concerning the Falling Asleep of Mary*, and *Pseudo-Melito*, most likely written in the fifth century. Both report that in response to Mary's prayer, all the disciples, living or dead, were miraculously reunited with her as she is prepared to die. Mary's importance to the early church is a subtheme of this image; she is the beloved Mother of Jesus and the beloved Mother of the Church.

The window that contains this scene, created between 1205 and 1215, addressed a debate that was taking place within the Western church in this period. No account of Mary's death is to be found in the canonical Scriptures, so medieval accounts of her death drew on apocryphal sources as well as their elaboration in legends. Thus theologians had different answers to the question "Did Mary die first and afterward was taken by the angels to heaven, or was she taken up into heaven without dying?" This image, along with others in this window that show her being placed in a casket and being carried to her tomb, demonstrate the answer at Chartres Cathedral. Theologians here taught that Mary did experience physical death. Only after dying was she assumed into heaven and reunited with her son.

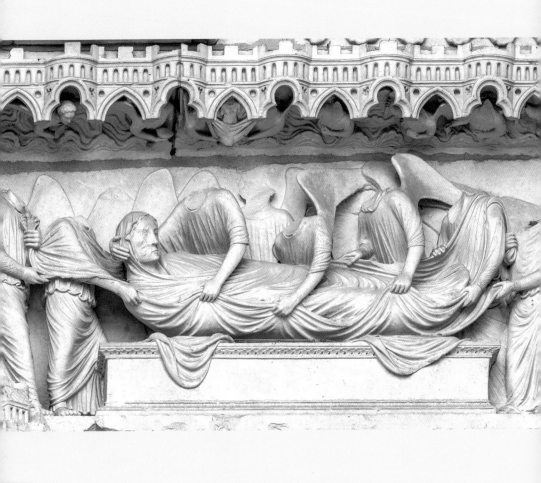

3.6 CARRIED BY ANGELS TO HEAVEN

Directly above the central North Porch doorways to the cathedral is a lintel with two scenes relating to the end of Mary's life. Her death is shown on the left, and her assumption on the right, where both her body (lower) and soul (upper row, small body) are being taken to heaven. These sculptural scenes were created and put in place between 1205 and 1230.

Here the angels are missing their heads, while the sculpture of Mary's extended, lifeless body remains intact. It was scaled larger than the angels' bodies to bring attention to her importance. The angels lift her from her sarcophagus, using the long fabric wrapping that covers her body. In medieval times care was taken not to touch anything sacred with one's hands, and this apparently held for the hands of angels, as well.

Above Mary, eight small angels' winged bodies emerge from the firmament. The one on the left still has its original head; the rest are headless. They all held objects at one time. Two bowls, probably used for holding incense, introduced in the early church as a liturgical symbol of cleansing and veneration, are still visible. The third and fourth angels from the left support a cloth out of which rises a naked, female torso representing Mary's soul. Like her body below, it is being lifted heavenward, where the two will be reunited.

What happened to Mary's flesh and bones after she died mattered at Chartres. The cult of relics that flourished in the Middle Ages depended on the bones of deceased saints. A belief in Mary's bodily assumption into heaven meant that relics that could connect people with her presence and power were limited almost exclusively to items that had touched her body, such as Mary's Veil that Charles the Bald had given to Chartres Cathedral in 876 (see pp. xxi, 79). The veil's special significance for clergy, parishioners, and pilgrims influenced the creation of many images at the cathedral, including this one.

3.7 THE ASSUMPTION OF MARY

This marble sculpture, weighing some thirty tons, is nineteen and a half feet tall and thirteen feet wide. It was created by Charles-Antoine Bridan, a well-respected French sculptor of his time. The church officially consecrated it in August of 1773. Mary, lifted by angels, is shown being raised above the clouds. Her face is turned upward; her arms are wide open. She appears to be in ecstasy as she anticipates reuniting with her son in heaven.

Mary, our Lady of the Assumption, is the patron saint of the Cathedral. Although the Catholic Church's dogma of the Assumption became official only in 1950, the Feast of the Assumption has been celebrated on August 15 in Chartres since the Middle Ages. It was one of the four days in the year that the liturgy focused on Mary. These feast days of Mary were also occasions for large fairs that brought many merchants and pilgrims to Chartres. Part of the medieval liturgy of Mary's assumption involved a public procession, probably both inside and outside the church. This tradition continues in modern times as parishioners and pilgrims process through Chartres singing and praying (see p. 96).

Bridan's monumental statue of Mary's assumption to heaven fills most of the front of the large cathedral choir and is visible even from the narthex in the west. One of the later additions to the cathedral's sculptural collection, the assumption of Mary evokes strong reactions. Some feel it is one of the most beautiful works of art in the cathedral; others believe the baroque work is out of place in a Gothic building. Regardless of one's opinion, its colossal size and central position in the sanctuary means that every visitor cannot help noticing it.

This work can inspire a desire to be united with Christ, as Mary his mother was. While her unique roles as Mother of Jesus, of God, and of the Church are understood to be unique, her longing for Christ, as so vividly expressed here, finds a resonance in many who take time to contemplate this sculptural grouping.

3.8 THE CROWNING OF MARY IN HEAVEN

Mary is clearly shown as the Queen of Heaven in both stained, glass and sculptural images at Chartres. This coronation of Mary image, created in the fifteenth century, reflects the striking emphasis on Mary's humility in the later Middle Ages. It is found on the south side of the nave in the Vendôme chapel. The window and chapel were gifts offered by Louis de Bourbon, the Count of Vendôme, a city located about fifty-six miles from Chartres. When Louis was imprisoned and threatened with death in 1413, he vowed to donate a chapel to the Virgin Mary should he ever be released. He kept his vow after leaving the prison; construction began at Chartres in 1417.

Christ is crowned and sits on his throne, resting his hand on a sizable globe that is topped with a cross. His regal red robe is trimmed with gold and lined with blue. King Jesus looks down at Mary and points to the two angels who are placing a pearl and jewel-studded crown on her head.

Mary kneels before Christ. She communicates her modesty and respect for him by crossing her arms over her chest and turning her eyes toward the floor. Her flowing golden hair shines against the backdrop of her red halo. A long blue cape, trimmed with gold, is draped over her shoulders and flows to the floor. There is no mistaking that Mary is a queen, and that she is subordinate to her son, Christ the King.

Images of Mary's coronation flowed from medieval beliefs about her body and soul's assumption into heaven after her death. When theologians imagined the reunion of Mary and her son in heaven, they spoke of the resurrected Christ crowning her. As this image shows, Mary no longer needed to wear the veil, for the emphasis on her role as terrestrial mother has changed to her fuller identity as the heavenly Queen and Mother of the Church.

3.9 MARY, THE INTERMEDIARY
TO THE SON OF GOD

Before passing through the central doors on the south porch and entering the cathedral, one can look up to contemplate sculptures related to the Last Judgment. On the tympanum Christ sits frontally, showing the five wounds of his crucifixion. On his right and left Mary and John, sitting on benches of the same height as Christ's, lean ever so slightly toward him and raise their hands in an easily recognizable position of prayer. Images of Mary at the final judgment were meant to reassure the faithful that through her prayers she would help them at the end of time.

Bishop Fulbert, in the sixth sermon on the Nativity of Mary that he preached in the eleventh century, and thus predating this thirteenth-century image, spoke to this need. "The more you see yourselves as guilty before the majesty of God, the more you should look to the Mother of the Lord, for she is full of mercy. You have an advocate with the Father, the Son of the Virgin himself, and he will be so kind with regard to your sins [cf. 1 John 2:1–2] that you may hope for forgiveness from him and from his Mother."

Modern viewers do well to remember the day-to-day reality of those who created and first contemplated this image, members of the strongly hierarchical feudal society of the late twelfth and early thirteenth centuries. When required to present a concern to someone in power, one sought an appropriate intermediary. This concept carried over into religious practice: few would dare to approach the King of Kings directly, relying rather on a mediator, someone who was respected and would have the ear of God and thus present their need for mercy in just the right way. Mary seemed to be the best choice possible. They reasoned that her son, the Son of God, would listen to what she had to say just as he had done at the wedding of Cana (see p. 28).

3.10 THE UBIQUITOUS SHIRT OF MARY

Most people standing at the west door of the North Porch don't notice the ancient iron keyhole shaped like a little shirt. It's not the only image of a small tunic at the cathedral. In fact, one could spend an entire day looking carefully at the windows, walls, furniture, and sculptures of the cathedral, and still not find them all! In addition to these, there are many other images of this "shirt" on the chalices, altar cloths, crosses, vestments, and other articles used in cathedral liturgies.

The significance of this symbol became apparent when a young tourist, whose accent revealed his Eastern European heritage, asked, "Where is Mary's T-shirt?" I had never heard the question before, so it gave me pause. I considered the various gift shops in town, and began giving him directions to the closest one. He looked quite confused. Then my husband asked, "Are you looking for the Veil of Mary?" "Yes, yes!" he replied.

In the sixteenth century, the clergy chose the shirt, a symbol of Mary's Holy Shirt as it was then called, to represent them. It still does today, decorating the bishop's pulpit, the rector's ceremonial cross, and the insignia that designates Chartres Cathedral as a basilica. Over the centuries this mark has been placed all through the cathedral. Its silent message is one of devotion, but also of ecclesiastical power.

From just before the year 1000 until the eighteenth century the veil was enclosed in a sealed cedar reliquary covered with gold; it was not visible from the outside. People assumed that what was then called the Holy Shirt (*Sainte Chemise* in French, or *Sancta Camisia* in Latin) or the Interior Tunic was an actual shirt. The reliquary held a long rectangular piece of silk, not a shirt. When this became known, the name of Mary's relic eventually changed to the Veil of Mary. However, the little short-sleeved-shirt symbol for the veil and for the cathedral chapter was not abandoned, as this keyhole and the other shirts around the church remind us.

## Chapter Four

MARY, MOTHER OF US ALL

4.1 INTRODUCTION

Blessed are you among women,
and blessed is the fruit of your womb.
And why has this happened to me,
that the mother of my Lord comes to me?
—LUKE 1:42–43

Mary is the Mother of Jesus and the Mother of all of us
even though it was Christ alone who reposed on her
knees. . . . If he is ours, we ought to be in his situation;
there where he is, we ought also to be and all that he has
ought to be ours, and his mother is also our mother.
—MARTIN LUTHER, 1529

4.2 PRAYING FOR A MOTHER'S TOUCH

Seeking help, comfort, and protection, many have come to Chartres Cathedral to pray near the Veil of Mary. Unlike most relics that link believers with the dead body of a saint, the veil is associated with Mary's and Jesus's live bodies since Mary is thought to have worn it during the Annunciation and Jesus's birth. Because Mary's body was believed to have been assumed to heaven after her death, people could only venerate relics linked to her life.

The history of this now fringed piece of silk, originally longer than seven feet, and about one and a half feet wide, is impossible to verify. It was a gift from French king Charles the Bald, whose grandfather Charlemagne was said to have received this precious cloth from Irene, the empress of the Byzantine Empire. Unfortunately, during the French Revolution, it was cut in pieces. Eventually, some of these, like the large fragment on display in the upper cathedral (see p. xxi), and the smaller displayed in the crypt (left), were returned to the cathedral.

Through the centuries there have been many claims of public and personal miracles associated with this veil. The most famous of these involves the routing of the troops of the Norman Viking king Rollo in 911 after Guillaume the bishop of Chartres exposed the veil above the city walls. After fire ravaged Chartres and its cathedral in 1194, the relic was carried intact from the ruins three days after the blaze. Hailed as a miracle, people interpreted this as a sign of Mary's favor. This enduring presence of Mary's Veil in Chartres motivated the construction of a larger and more beautiful "home" for Notre-Dame de Chartres. Miracles of protection during battles for men, and during childbirth for women, were reported through the centuries by those wearing a small piece of cloth or metal that had been held against the reliquary that housed the veil.

Pilgrims from all over the world still come to pray before the veil, seeking Mary's compassionate aid. Many continue to speak of the answers to their prayers.

4.4 MARY'S ADVICE

A small scene of Mary and two servants found near the bottom of the Blue Virgin Window depicts an important part of the story of the wedding at Cana (John 2:1–11). Mary, identified by her halo and the small cross on the veil above her forehead, is taller and thus visually and symbolically more significant than the two servants. She holds a blue book under her arm, close to her body. As in other images, this represents Mary's willingness to carry the Word of God.

Clothed in green and red tunics, the two servants hold water jugs. The stylized cloud above their heads lets the viewer know that the scene is taking place outside. The man closest to Mary is engaged in conversation with her, his hand suggesting a receptivity to what she is saying.

Mary speaks in only three biblical stories. Luke records her words in the presence of the angel Gabriel at the Annunciation, and during the Visitation after Elizabeth has greeted her. John, in his Gospel, also quotes Mary during the account of the marriage feast at Cana. After declaring that "they have no [more] wine," Mary summarizes her trust and faith in Jesus using five words to the servants: "Do whatever [Jesus] tells you" (John 2:5).

In this image, the man dressed in red is turned toward the next pane, suggesting that he is already moving toward Jesus, who will give him instructions to "fill the [empty] jars [for the Jewish rite of purification] with water" (2:6).

The position of Mary's body, facing not the servant but the viewers, suggests that this message is not only for them, but for all. Her right palm is open, a hand position that often represents acceptance, as one finds in many Annunciation scenes where Mary's "Yes" to God changed the course of history.

The message of this image is clear: doing God's will is the duty not only of these servants but of all who follow Christ. Mary is showing that others should follow her words and her example.

4.5 INSPIRED TO BUILD MARY'S HOME

History and legend are sometimes difficult to separate, especially when considering the medieval Cult of the Carts. It is reported that love for Mary inspired a great outpouring of devotion prompting men and women of all social classes to give of themselves in building the Chartres Cathedral. Several accounts of such outpourings of popular piety exist; the first was reported to have occurred in the mid-twelfth century and another after a fire destroyed the church in 1194. References to the confession of sins, singing of hymns, recitation of prayers, times of reverential silence, granting of forgiveness, and true repentance exist in accounts describing what took place as people, acting as beasts of burden, brought needed building supplies to Chartres on carts.

While these images may depict workers bringing items to sell, many scholars think they show some of the thousands of people who are reported to have hauled wagons to express their need for forgiveness, their desire to serve God, or their hope to please Mary by being a part of building a cathedral worthy of her. In front of the carts on both sides of the window, men lean forward under the strain of pulling the wagons. At least seven can be seen on the left, two in the far circle and five or six more in front of them in the central circle. On the right, two men pull the wagon. The carts are loaded high, with sacks of supplies on the left, and a large barrel on the right.

In the center of the image is a statue of Mary and Jesus at the cathedral, with a basket for donations underneath. Many pray nearby, including a small kneeling boy who holds up two crutches, demonstrating Mary's ability to heal pilgrims who work or pray at the cathedral. The desired connection between offerings of physical labor, spiritual worship, and monetary gifts shines brightly in this stained-glass window dedicated to the miracles of Mary.

4.6 MARY SAVES THEOPHILUS

Four images in the Miracles of Mary Window show scenes taken from the popular medieval legend and liturgical drama of Mary's saving Theophilus (meaning "one who loves God") from the devil. The story is told of Theophilus, a priest and the assistant to a bishop. When the man's superior died, church authorities invited this priest to become the new bishop. Theophilus, not feeling worthy of the episcopacy, asked that he not be appointed. The authorities acquiesced and chose another candidate. The new bishop, for reasons that were not revealed, quickly dismissed Theophilus.

Being infuriated by this injustice, Theophilus gave up his life of holiness and signed a pact with the devil. In return for renouncing his belief in God, Christ, and Mary, the devil enabled him to go back to his former position of power. Eventually, he felt so guilty about what he had done that he entered a chapel dedicated to Mary, and begged her to help him. She came to him in a vision, and after rebuking him, made him confess Jesus as the Son of God. Then, in a parallel to the creedal claim that Jesus "descended to hell," Mary also went to hell, as represented by the flaming open mouth on the left side of the image. In the stained-glass image of her recovering the document from the devil, she stands above him, manifesting the superiority of her power. After recovering the agreement signed by Theophilus, she placed the pact on the sleeping man's chest, thereby assuring him that he was free.

Many medieval windows, sculptures, and manuscripts include the story of Theophilus. At Chartres, Bishop Fulbert (d. 1028) also used it as an illustration in a sermon given on the Feast of Mary's Nativity. This legend, full of instruction on the need to resist temptation, the possibility of forgiveness, and how to receive help out of seemingly disastrous situations was meant to encourage faithful living. It also inspired confidence in Mary's capability of aiding those who were wanting to turn back to God.

4.7 A MOTHER'S TOUCHING GRIEF

Mary is identifiable by her position next to her crucified son on his right side (our left), as well as by the small brown cross in the center of her veil. This image, from the mid-twelfth century, depicts a faithful mother in deep grief. The tenderness of her touch is almost palpable as the viewer notices how she has placed her hands behind the limp hands of her dead son while drawing one to rest against her cheek.

Mary hangs on to Jesus's lifeless hands while his body is being removed from the cross. Although its green core symbolizes the life Christ's death will bring to his followers, the red outline reminds the viewer of the bloody ordeal that Jesus was made to suffer. His mother's red halo, sleeves, and inner garment remind those who contemplate this image that she, too, is suffering after the bloody crucifixion. The prophecy of Simeon at the dedication of Jesus in the temple (see p. 25) rings true: "a sword will pierce your own soul too" (Luke 2:35). Mary's slumped body, her furrowed brow, and sad eyes express her sorrow.

This image may have had a particular significance at Chartres. A thirteenth-century document, *The Miracles of Our Lady of Chartres*, translated into French by Jean Le Marchant from an earlier Latin text, describes seven different mothers crying out to Mary to save their children who had either died or were about to die. Five were resurrected, and the other two were healed. These stories suggest the trust mothers placed in Mary, a mother who herself had endured the death of her child, and whose compassion, when called on at Chartres, was powerfully efficacious.

4.9 A GRATEFUL KING'S VOW

The Vow of King Louis XIII, in which he dedicated his kingdom to Mary, is the subject of a marble bas-relief on the south wall of the inner choir. Like the large sculpture of Mary's assumption (see p. 66), it was sculpted by Charles-Antoine Bridan in 1788. Louis XIII, who reigned in France from 1610 to 1643, is shown on his knees holding out his crown toward Mary and Jesus, who sit in the clouds. Mary holds her naked child securely with her left arm and hand while displaying an open-palmed right hand that is turned toward the king and his gift. Jesus's arms are also wide open to the king and his crown as well. Both Mary and Jesus gaze at King Louis, who is looking up to them. A soldier stands behind him, keeping guard. Four other well-dressed men behind these two look toward Mary and Jesus; their bodies communicate their deep respect for them, as well as their support of the king.

When Louis XIII's wife, Anne of Austria, became pregnant after over twenty years of infertility, he submitted a document to the Parliament on February 10, 1638, in which he dedicated the kingdom of France to Mary. He also decreed that any church that was not already dedicated to Mary should set aside its main chapel to honor her. Finally, he declared that in order that his subjects properly celebrate the Feast of Mary's Assumption, annual processions should take place in every diocese in France on August 15.

A reading of the vow of Louis XIII takes place at Chartres Cathedral each August 15, during a ceremony that includes the Consecration of France to Mary. The heart of his edict rings out, "Very Holy Virgin Mary . . . , today we renew before you the solemn consecration [of France by Louis XIII] and we dedicate ourselves, our families, our country, all that we have and are to you."

4.10 SHARING THE JOY AND GRIEF
OF MOTHERHOOD

Tenderness and connection radiate from these twelfth-century sculptures of Mary and her kinswoman Elizabeth, who proclaims: "Blessed are you among women and blessed is the fruit of your womb." They are shown holding hands, with Elizabeth's arm wrapping around Mary's shoulder affectionately. Their heads lean ever so slightly toward each other. The closeness of their bodies recalls their shared lineage, faith, and experience of God's incarnation as described in the Visitation text (see Luke 1:39–56). Standing side by side, these two pregnant women carry hope. Elizabeth's son, John the Baptist, will "prepare the way of the LORD" (Isaiah 40:3; Matthew 3:3), and Mary's son, Jesus, will be the Messiah (Luke 2:8–11).

The Cathedral of Notre-Dame de Chartres, although dedicated to Mary, has honored John the Baptist as its second patron since the Middle Ages. Both Elizabeth's son, John, and Mary shared the mission of pointing others to Jesus. John stated this clearly: "He must increase, but I must decrease" (John 3:30). The Visitation images at the cathedral highlight the connection between Mary and John, even if John, still developing in his mother's womb, is not yet visible.

The contemplative nature of Elizabeth's and Mary's expressions might be understood as foreshadowing future pain, since their mothers' hearts, so full of promise at the Visitation, would both experience the grief of having their sons murdered. Mary, here shown with a halo and crown, is clearly singled out as the one that all generations will henceforth call blessed (Luke 1:48). At the same time, her closeness to Elizabeth reminds viewers of her approachability, in times of both joy and sorrow.

Chapter Five

MARY AT CHARTRES IN THE TWENTY-FIRST CENTURY

5.1 INTRODUCTION

"Who are my mother and my brothers?"
And looking at those who sat around him, he said,
"Here are my mother and my brothers!
Whoever does the will of God is my brother
and sister and mother."

—MARK 3:33–35

5.2 MARY, MOTHER OF THE SON OF JUSTICE

The towers of Chartres Cathedral, pointing heavenward with beauty and strength, can be seen across the fields from miles away. At closer range, a sun-shaped weather vane is clearly visible, as is the cross that sits directly below it on the north tower. Gracing the base of the cross is a copper image of Mary holding an oversized baby Jesus. It is far too high to be seen from the ground, but its presence is not diminished by a lack of visibility.

Mary, a young woman clothed in a flowing dress, holds her naked infant son on her right side. She looks toward the cherublike Jesus, her extended left hand wrapping around his body in a maternally protective way. Jesus playfully runs both his hands through his mother's long veil as it shields him from behind. He is safe and secure.

In the late seventeenth century, after hurricanelike winds caused damage to the cross on the north tower's spire, a metal base weighing over half a ton was added for support. This image of Mary and Jesus was placed on one side, while the other had an inscription describing the repair work that had been undertaken. Snakes circle the very bottom of the bulbous support where Mary's foot crushes one of the serpents, recalling Genesis 3:15.

A sun weather vane with Christ blessing in the center moves back and forth above the image of Mary and Jesus. An inscription on one side of the sun reads, "Jesus, son of Justice, have mercy on your people." The text on the other side is, "I am the light of the world; I give you my peace." The image of Mary and Jesus adds to this blessing being sent out from atop the cathedral. Though seen only occasionally by workers, this image of Our Lady of Chartres, caring for her son and fighting back the forces of evil, is a reminder that she will also use her maternal love to protect and bless those who have found their way to the cathedral.

5.3 MARY, A MOTHER WHO HAS SUFFERED

This distressing image showing the massacre of the innocents depicts the murder of infant boys and the inconsolable grief of their mothers (Matthew 2:16–18). The mother on the left looks into the eyes of a soldier with a sword raised over his head, while trying to pull her child away from him. At the bottom of the image, next to two naked, decapitated bodies, a grief-stricken mother holds her son's severed head as she looks with sadness at his dead face.

Mary's ability to relate to mothers of murdered or deceased children might explain the inclusion of this story in a window dedicated to the life of the mother of Jesus. While Mary and her son escaped his demise by Herod during their flight to Egypt, before the end of Jesus's life, Mary had to watch as soldiers crucified her son. As such, the story is an important chapter of the Christmas narrative, celebrated liturgically from antiquity on December 28, a reminder of children's vulnerability and the senseless violence sometimes exercised against them.

The suffering that Mary endured has inspired others, overcome with pain, to trust her ability to accompany them through their unspeakable grief. Throughout the centuries, many mothers and fathers have brought their needy children and their broken hearts to Chartres Cathedral, asking for Mary's help. These mothers still come. After her daughter was murdered during the terrorist attack in Paris at the Bataclan Theater in November 2015, one such mother from Chartres came to pray at the cathedral during her funeral.

In these challenging and violent times, images like this one, placed in the larger narrative about Mary, remind modern viewers that they can share their greatest trials and injustices with Mary and Christ Jesus. They had to endure the worst of humanity themselves. Yet they also experienced the resurrection power of God, which did not take the horror away, but helped to place it in a much larger context.

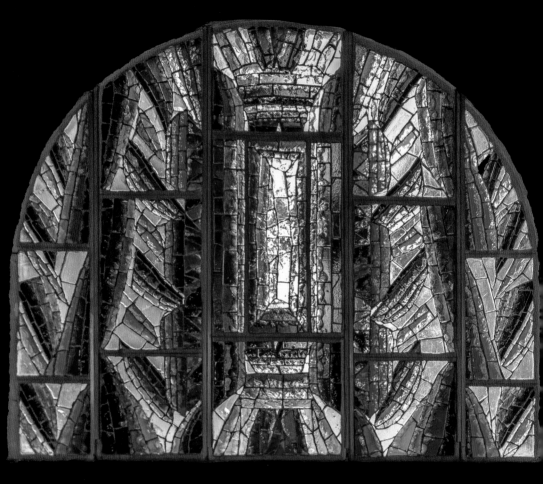

5.4 THE ONGOING STORY OF MARY

The stained-glass window called Mary, Doorway to Heaven, evokes emotion and stimulates the mind. It is a modern, figurative interpretation of Mary that expresses the same key messages and Marian elements found elsewhere in the cathedral. Installed on the Feast of the Annunciation in 2010, and dedicated by Bishop Michel Pansard a year later, this is the cathedral's newest stained-glass window.

Replacing a wall that had sealed an old entryway to the crypt for centuries, the window is found to the left as one looks at the altar in the chapel of *Notre-Dame de Sous-Terre*. This luminous blue creation, the final work of well-known French artist Henri Guérin, shows how modern devotion to Mary fits seamlessly with that of the millions of pilgrims who over many centuries have visited this ancient Marian chapel and the cathedral that houses it.

Placed above nine steps that suggest the nine lines of Mary's Magnificat, the window evokes many Marian stories and themes. Guérin created the central doorway to suggest God's light coming into Mary's life and womb at the Annunciation. He imagined a two-way portal, describing the center as also representing Mary's Assumption when she joined her son after death.

While the window's colors and title bring focus to Mary, the incarnation, crucifixion, and resurrection of her son also shine forth from this window. Guérin placed red on each side of the doorway to evoke Christ's passion. He used both color and line in the central three panels to express that Christ's resurrection permanently opened the passageway to and from God.

In art, liturgy, and the lives of those who pray, devotion to Mary and her son continues at Chartres Cathedral.

EPILOGUE

Outside the Pillar Chapel, a large clear receptacle (42 inches high by 34 inches long by 28 inches wide) with blank papers and a chained-on pen awaits those who would like to share a written expression of their heart with Mary. Note by note, the box fills with thousands of handwritten pleas that most likely represent every type of suffering, longing, and emotion that humans know. When there is no more room inside, all the papers from this repository are taken to a local women's monastery where all they represent is committed to God's loving care.

Visiting Chartres Cathedral with its ancient and modern images offers far more than the opportunity to appreciate the finest and most complete collection of medieval stained-glass windows in the world. This building that is dedicated to God and the veneration of Mary opens its doors to the sacred possibility of connecting one's deepest human longings with the loving care of God each day of every year. While people enter to look, reflect, search, and learn, many also come to pray.

The ancient stone pillar under the statue of *Notre-Dame du Pilier* often feels cold to the hand as it is touched at the end of one's prayers. At the same time, the warm light from the colored glass above supports visitors, parishioners, and pilgrims as they open to something greater than themselves. It is impossible to imagine just how many millions of people have brought their troubled, grateful, or longing hearts and shared them with Mary and her son here.

Pilgrims continue to come to Chartres. Some communicate with God or Mary silently, some pray together out loud, some sit in quiet contemplation, and others to move from chapel to chapel, lighting candles and reciting prayers. Each is like a strand of fiber in an immense tapestry that is woven not by their efforts, but by the unseen, creative hand of God. Its invisible beauty is far more glorious than that of any of the masterpieces already found in the cathedral. This work of art, begun when the first person came to reach out to Christ and his mother, will not be fully finished or appreciated until it is viewed from the heavenly Jerusalem that this cathedral was built to represent.

DEDICATION AND ACKNOWLEDGMENTS

I dedicate this book to all who come to Chartres Cathedral seeking to know God better and serve Christ more faithfully. As you absorb God's love here, may the words and images on these pages encourage you personally, while inspiring you to make our world more the just, beautiful, caring place we long for it to be.

Special thanks to the three people who have helped the most:

Timothy Clarence Geoffrion, my husband and ministry partner, who has always supported my work in Chartres, even when it has meant long absences or missed opportunities to work together. For your careful reading and responses to each page of this book, for your encouragement of me as an artist, for your faithful prayers for me and this work, and for all the ways in which your love has made this possible, I am deeply grateful.

Alain Pierre Robert Louët, the colleague with whom I have been studying Mary in Chartres Cathedral for the past nine years. For our countless discussions, the responses to the multitude of my questions, the sharing of resources in French, and the many expressions of help and friendship, I am deeply grateful.

Mark Burrows, my editor, who has thoughtfully accompanied me as the book idea developed and came to life. For your great questions, incredible knowledge, and sense of beauty, I am deeply grateful.

I also express my deep gratitude to:

My "Mary Friends," in Chartres and across the globe: Annonciade, Bénédicte Bouillot, Linda Campbell, Michelle Campbell, Felicity Collins, Cheryl Felicia Dudley, Sara Jane Kingston, Lucie, Mary Jean McGregor, Jan Neville, Mary Kaye Medinger, Kimberly Lowelle Saward, and each of the members of the Chemin Neuf community with whom I have sung Mary's Song at Vespers during the last sixteen years. Thank you for the talks we've had, the questions you've asked, the books you've suggested, the feedback you've given, the encouragement you've shared, the prayers you've prayed on my behalf, and our shared prayer.

My "Chartres friends," including many family members, with whom I've spend time in the cathedral and who have helped me to improve the manuscript, each in her or his unique way:

Judith Doré, Robert Ferré, Daniel Eugene Geoffrion, Ken Geoffrion, Timothy Charles Geoffrion, Lucy Hartwell, and Stella Wang. Thank you for taking time together to share the beauty and prayer environment of Chartres Cathedral. Thank you for being willing to make what was important to me important to you.

Those who have helped me out of their deep knowledge and commitment to Chartres Cathedral: Helge Burggrabe, John James, Irène Jourd'heuil, Dominique Lallement, Malcolm Miller, and Msgr. Michel Pansard.

WORKS CITED IN THE TEXT (IN ORDER)

PROLOGUE

Bernard of Clairvaux, quotation from *Hom. II super Missus est* 17 (*PL* 183:70–71), quoted by Pope Benedict XVI. Translation by *L'Osservatore Romano*, October 28, 2009, 24, https://www.ewtn.com/library/PAPALDOC /b16ChrstChrch93.htm

Bernard's dedication to Mary, like Chartres's Bishop Fulbert before him (d. 1028), had a major impact on the church of his day.

PREFACE

Yves Delaporte, *Les trois Notre-Dame de la cathédrale de Chartres: études suivie de la liste des images de la Vierge appartenant à la cathédrale et de quelques mots sur le pèlerinage de Chartres* (Chartres: Éditions Houvet, 1955), 80–94.

INTRODUCTION TO CHAPTER 4

Martin Luther, *Christmas Sermon*, 1529.

Vatican, *Catechism of the Catholic Church*, part I, section 2, chapter 3, article 9, para. 6, "Mary - Mother of Christ, Mother of the Church," 963–75. The quote is from 973.

APPENDIX ONE

Dates and window scene numbers were almost exclusively found at Chartres: Cathedral of Notre-Dame, Digital Research Library, University of Pittsburgh, http://images.library.pitt.edu/c/chartres/.

Map of the Architectural Features of the Upper Church (p. 122)

Map of the Crypt of Chartres Cathedral (p. 123)

APPENDIX TWO

Adapted from Eugène-Emmanuel Viollet-le-Duc, *Dictionnaire raisonné de l'architecture française du XIe au XVIe siècle* (Paris : A. Morel, 1856), tome 2 [312], figure 11.

Adapted from Marcel-Joseph Bulteau, *Description de la cathédrale de Chartres suivie d'une courte notice sur les églises de Saint-Pierre, de Saint-André et de Saint-Aignan de la même ville avec cinq planches* (Chartres: Garnier, 1850), between 268 and 269.

Stones, Allison. Chartres: Cathedral of Notre-Dame—Digital Research Library. University of Pittsburgh, Pennsylvania. http://images.library .pitt.edu/c/chartres/. Accessed May 9, 2016.

Wright, Wendy M. *Mary and the Catholic Imagination: Le Point Vierge.* The Madeleva Lecture in Spirituality. Mahwah, NJ: Paulist Press, 2010.

POUR LES PERSONNES QUI LISENT LE FRANÇAIS

Ces livres sont essentiels pour mieux comprendre Marie, Notre-Dame de Chartres.

Balzano, Nicolas. *Les deux cathédrales mythe et histoire à Chartres, XIe-XXe siècle, Vérité des mythes.* Paris: les Belles lettres, 2012.

Bulteau, Marcel-Joseph. *Description de la cathédrale de Chartres suivie d'une courte notice sur les églises de Saint-Pierre, de Saint-André et de Saint-Aignan de la même ville avec cinq planches.* Chartres : Garnier, 1850.

Delaporte, Yves. *Les trois Notre-Dame de la cathédrale de Chartres : études suivie de la liste des images de la Vierge appartenant à la cathédrale et de quelques mots sur le pèlerinage de Chartres.* Chartres : Éditions Houvet, 1955.

Dombes, Groupe des. *Marie dans le dessein de Dieu et la communion des saints I : dans l'histoire et l'Écriture.* Paris : Bayard Éditions, 1977.

———. *Marie dans le dessein de Dieu et la communion des saints II : controverse et conversion.* Paris : Bayard Éditions, 1998.

James, John. *Chartres, les constructeurs.* Chartres : Société archéologique d'Eure-et-Loir, 1977.

Jouanneaux, Françoise. *Décor et mobilier : Cathédrale Notre-Dame de Chartres.* Orléans, France : Inventaire Général du Patrimoine Culturel, 2008.

Lautier, Claudine. *Les vitraux de la cathédrale de Chartres : Reliques et images.* Paris : Société Française d'Archéologie, 2003.

Mâle, Émile. *Notre-Dame de Chartres.* Traduit de Sarah Wilson. Paris: Flammarion, 1963.

Marchant, Jean le. *Miracles de Notre-Dame de Chartres*. Chartres : Société Archéologique d'Eure-et-Loir, 1973.

Musée des Beaux-Arts de Chartres. *Trésors de la Cathédrale de Chartres*. Deauville : Illustria, 2002.

Pansard, Michel, François Delaunay, Henri Gaud, et Arnaud Hébert. *Chartres sous la direction de Mgr. Michel Pansard direction scientifique et coordination, Jean-Paul Deremble, Gilles Fresson, Jean-François Lagier. [et al.] [Photographies, François Delaunay, Henri Gaud, Arnaud Hébert], La grâce d'une cathédrale*. Strasbourg [Paris] : la Nuée bleue, 2013.

Prache, Anne, et Pascale Etchecopar. *Notre-Dame de Chartres : Image de la Jérusalem céleste*. Illustrations, Pascale Etchecopar. [Nouvelle éd.] ed, *Patrimoine*. Paris: CNRS éd., 2008.

SIGNIFICANT ARCHITECTURAL ELEMENTS OF CHARTRES CATHEDRAL

PART 1: DEFINITION OF TERMS

ambulatory A place for walking, especially an aisle around the apse or a cloister in a church or monastery. The double ambulatory at Chartres circles the outside of the choir.

apse Semicircular or polygonal termination to the choir or sanctuary. Occasionally it is located at the end of an aisle.

cathedral A church that serves as the central church in a diocese. It contains the "seat" (*sedes*) of the bishop.

capstone One of the finishing stones that holds the vault together. Sometimes these stones are sculpted and serve a decorative purpose. In French: *clef de voûte*.

chalice A cup to hold wine used for the Eucharist.

choir The part of a church between the high altar and the nave, generally used by the choir and clergy. It is often separated from the nave by steps or a screen.

ciborium A cup-shaped container that has a cover. Its purpose is to hold the Eucharistic Hosts.

clerestory The upper part of a church, higher than the flanking aisles, that allows light in through its windows.

cruciform Having the shape of a cross; many medieval cathedrals, including Chartres, were built using the shape of a cross including a nave, choir, and transept.

Gothic architecture	Having evolved from Romanesque architecture (below), it is characterized by ogival (pointed) arches, ribbed vaults, and buttresses. The search for height and light were made possible by these features of the new building style.
lancet	Resembling the shape of a lance, a tall, narrow window that is pointed on the top.
lintel	A horizontal support across the top of a door often used as a place to display small sculptural scenes.
nave	The central area of a church building (from the Latin for "ship").
paten	A plate used during the Eucharistic meal.
porch	An architectural feature that extends from the side of a church that both protects the entrance(s) and is often used as an area to illustrate truths of the faith in sculpture. Chartres Cathedral has three porches (west, north, and south).
Romanesque architecture	Characterized by semicircular arches, this building style was also known for thick walls and groin vaults. It eventually developed into the Gothic style (above). Although dates for this period vary, it is generally considered to have flourished between the tenth and twelfth centuries in Europe.
rood screen	*Rood* is an old English word for cross. A separating wall between the nave and choir of a church. At Chartres, the medieval rood screen was made of stone. The rood screen technically separates the sanctuary, where the Eucharist is celebrated around the altar, from the nave where the worshipers gathered.
sarcophagus	A stone coffin
socle	A support serving as the base for something rising above.

transept   The part of a church that lies across the main area of the building. At Chartres, with its cruciform design, the transept forms the arms of the cross.

trumeau   A central pillar that divides a large doorway. When used in church buildings, it often supports the tympanum above a doorway. Often it is decorated with sculptures.

tympanum   A half-moon space above the lintel over a doorway. It is typically decorated with sculpture.

Appendix Two

IMAGES FOUND AT CHARTRES CATHEDRAL

PART 1: TABLE OF IMAGES USED

All photographs were taken by the author, unless noted. Numbers before each entry correspond to section numbers and the locations of the images on the cathedral and crypt maps.

PAGE #	TITLE OF ENTRY	NAME OF IMAGE	DESCRIPTION	LOCATION/MATERIAL/DATE
C	Cover	The Blue Virgin Window	Mary's and Jesus's upper bodies	South ambulatory Stained glass, 1180
FRONT MATTER				
Title		Chartres Cathedral	The West Facade	Chartres, France
xi		Worship at Chartres	The Chrismal Service	The altar in the crossing taken from the north triforium
PROLOGUE				
xii	Prologue	Miracle of the milk of Mary	Bishop Fulbert lying on his deathbed being visited by the healing presence of Mary	South transept (lower east side) Fulbert Stained glass, 1954

# ON MAP	TITLE OF ENTRY	NAME OF IMAGE	DESCRIPTION	LOCATION/MATERIAL/DATE
FOREWORD				
xiv	Foreword	Monseigneur Michel Pansard, Bishop of Chartres	Blessing of the palms on Palm Sunday	Bishop's Garden (behind the cathedral) 21st century
xvii	Foreword	The Annunciation	Gabriel and Mary	Lintel of south doorway of west wall, Sculpture 1145
PREFACE				
xviii	Preface	Gabriel announcing the incarnation of Jesus to Mary	Detail from the Annunciation (Gabriel is not shown)	West wall Life of Christ Stained glass 1145–55
xxi	Preface	Stained glass windows, the Veil of Mary	Evening view of the Heart of Mary Chapel	North ambulatory and chapel, Stained glass 13th century Silk, 1st century
xxii	Preface	Marguerite of Lèves, Mary, Jesus	Marguerite of Lèves, one of the donors of this window. Her husband is in the scene to the right.	South ambulatory Saint Margaret and Saint Catherine window Stained glass 1220–27
xxv	Preface	Mary, Jesus, Jill on a scaffold during restorations ©Alain Pierre Louët	Mary, Throne of Wisdom, with Jesus on her lap, Jill	Central window of upper choir, top image Stained glass 1210–25
INTRODUCTION: MARY, OUR LADY OF CHARTRES				
xxvi	Introduction	Chartres Cathedral	A winter view of the cathedral looking toward the west wall	Gothic cathedral, 13th century
2	Introduction	The Presentation of Jesus in the Temple	Mary and Jesus look at each other	South ambulatory Life of Mary Stained Glass, 1217–20
5	Introduction	Our Lady of the Crypt	Jesus on his mother's lap	Crypt Notre-Dame de Sous-Terre Wood statue, 1976
6	Introduction	The burial of Jesus	Mary (top left) witnessing the entombment of her son	Southwest wall The passion of Christ Stained glass 1145–55

# ON MAP	TITLE OF ENTRY	NAME OF IMAGE	DESCRIPTION	LOCATION/MATERIAL/DATE
			CHAPTER ONE: MARY, MOTHER OF JESUS	
8	Introduction	Flight to Egypt: Joseph, Mary, Jesus	Mary, Jesus gazing into each other's eyes	South ambulatory, Life of Mary Stained glass 1217–20
10	Introduction	The Nativity	Mary, Jesus, Angels, Joseph	Outer choir, south side Sculpture, Jehan Soulas 1521–1535
12	Mary, Descendant of King David	The Jesse Tree Window Detail of Mary with Isaiah (left) and Daniel (right)	Old Testament ancestry of Jesus flanked by prophets	West wall Tree of Jesse Stained glass 1145–55
15	Mary, Daughter of Anne	Anne and Mary	Standing Anne holding her daughter with her left arm	North wall central lancet (D) Stained glass, 1235
16	Mary and the Word of God	Mary at School	Teacher and students; Mary reading a book	South ambulatory, Life of Mary, Stained glass 1217–20
18	Directing Others to Jesus	The Annunciation	Gabriel and Mary with the dove (Holy Spirit) entering her halo	Upper choir, east Stained glass, 1210–25
21	From Her Womb: A King Is Born	The Nativity	Mary, Jesus, Joseph an ox, a donkey, and the star announcing Jesus's birth	West wall, Life of Christ Stained glass, 1145–55
22	Pondering the Mystery	The Nativity	Mary, Joseph, Jesus	Rood screen currently in storage, Bas-relief ca. 1230–40
25	Offering Her Son to God	The Presentation of Jesus at the Temple	Mary, Jesus, and Simeon during Jesus's Presentation	West wall, Life of Christ Stained glass, 1145–55
26	Safely in Her Arms	The Flight to Egypt	Joseph, Mary, and Jesus traveling to Egypt, God's hand emerging from the cloud	South upper choir, westernmost window, top pane, Nativity and Flight to Egypt, Stained glass 1210–25
28	A Mother's Influence	The Wedding of Cana. The story reads from left to right and from bottom to top.	Mary and Jesus talk with each other	South ambulatory Blue Virgin, bottom six scenes, Stained glass 1215–20

# ON MAP	TITLE OF ENTRY	NAME OF IMAGE	DESCRIPTION	LOCATION/MATERIAL/DATE
68	The Crowning of Mary in Heaven	Coronation of Mary	Christ on a throne, Mary kneeling, angels holding a crown over her head	South aisle nave Vendôme chapel Stained glass 1415 and Modern
71	Mary, the Intermediary to the Son of God	Intercession at the Final Judgment	Mary, Jesus, John	South porch, Tympanum of the central doorway Sculpture, 1194–1230
73	The Ubiquitous Shirt of Mary	Keyhole in the shape of a shirt	Mary's shirt, the symbol of Mary's Veil and of the chapter of the cathedral	North porch, west door Iron keyhole, 16th or 17th century
CHAPTER FOUR: MARY, MOTHER OF US ALL				
74	Introduction	Dedicating baptized children to the Virgin Mary	Prayer near Notre-Dame du Pilier	North Ambulatory, Notre Dame du Pilier Chapel 2016
76	Introduction	Brass and gold hearts offered to Mary	Hearts offered to Mary	Many are in a safe location; others can be seen in the Pillar Chapel Copper, some with gold 19th–20th centuries
78	Praying for a Mother's Touch	The small piece of the Veil of Mary	Reliquary for the small piece of the Veil of Mary	Crypt, south arm of the Notre-Dame de Sous-Terre Chapel, Reliquary 1822, Silk 1st century
80	The Blessed Milk of the Mother	Mary holding out her bare breast to Jesus	Mary, Jesus, two angels	South ambulatory, small rose above the Blue Virgin Stained glass, 1215–20
83	Mary's Advice	The Wedding at Cana	Mary instructing two servants who are holding pitchers	South ambulatory, Bottom of the Blue Virgin, stained glass, 1215–20
84	Inspired to Build Mary's Home	The Cult of the Carts	Pulling wagons of supplies to Chartres, pilgrims praying near a statue of Mary and Jesus	South aisle of the nave The miracles of Mary Stained glass, 1205–15
86	Mary Saves Theophilus	Mary receiving a document with Theophilus's vow from the devil	Mary, the devil, the flaming mouth of hell	South aisle of the nave The miracles of Mary Stained glass, 1205–15
89	A Mother's Touching Grief	The deposition of Jesus from the cross with Mary holding his hands in hers	Mary, Jesus, John, Nicodemus and Joseph of Arimathea removing Jesus's body from the cross	Southwest wall, The passion of Christ, Stained glass, 1145–55

# ON MAP	TITLE OF ENTRY	NAME OF IMAGE	DESCRIPTION	LOCATION/MATERIAL/DATE
91	Donors' Devotion to Mary	Throne of Wisdom	Mary, Jesus, a man and woman donor from Tours	North upper clerestory, next to the transept small rose, Stained glass 1210–25
92	A Grateful King's Vow	King Louis XIII offers his crown to Mary	King Louis XIII, soldier, witnesses, Mary, and Jesus	South inner choir, Marble bas-relief, 1788, Bridan
94	Sharing the Joy and Grief of Motherhood	The Visitation	Elizabeth (left) and Mary (right) holding each other	West wall, lower lintel over the south doorway Sculpture, ca. 1145

CHAPTER FIVE: MARY AT CHARTRES IN THE TWENTY-FIRST CENTURY				
96	Introduction	Mary procession in Chartres on the Feast of the Assumption	*Notre-Dame du Pilier* being carried by pilgrims and parishioners	Outside the west central doors of the cathedral Clothed wooden statue 1508 Procession 21st century
98	Introduction	Priest with Marian imagery on his chasuble	Discussion after the Paschal Vigil near the crossing	Fabric, Embroidered image of the center of the North rose, 21st century
100	Mary, Mother of the Son of Justice	Mother and son	Mary holding naked infant Jesus	North tower, base of the cross Modern mold of the 1692 metal original; Sun, Christ blessing, cross, and top of north tower 1692
103	Mary, a Mother Who Has Suffered	The Massacre of the Innocents	Soldiers, mothers, dead, naked children	South ambulatory, Life of Mary, Stained glass 1217–20
104	The Ongoing Story of Mary	Mary, the Gateway to Heaven *Marie, Porte du Ciel*	Figurative doorway showing Mary and Christ's experiences of God	Crypt: *Notre-Dame de Sous-Terre* Chapel (northeast end) Mary, Gateway to Heaven Stained glass, 2010

EPILOGUE				
106	Epilogue	Prayer, touching the pillar on which Notre-Dame du Pilier is placed	Pilgrim, statue and pillar	North Ambulatory Pillar Chapel 21st century
109	Epilogue	Cantor, Paschal Vigil	Member of the Chemin Neuf Community	Altar area Central Crossing 2017

# ON MAP	TITLE OF ENTRY	NAME OF IMAGE	DESCRIPTION	LOCATION/MATERIAL/DATE
DEDICATION AND ACKNOWLEDGMENTS				
110	Before Dedication and Acknowledg-ments	The Adoration of the Magi	Jesus and his mother (Magi not shown)	Outer choir, South Ambulatory Jean Soulas, 1521-1535
APPENDICES				
116	Selected Bibliography	Iconic Face of Mary	Mary looking at Jesus (not shown) who is interacting with a Wise Man (not shown)	South Ambulatory Life of Mary Stained glass 1217-1220
124	Appendix Two	Notre-Dame du Pilier	Mary and Jesus	Procession, August 15th 21st century
133	Images Found at Chartres Cathedral	The Nave looking west from the altar area	Cathedral lit in candlelight	21st century
136	Table of Marian Imagery	St. Anne holding young Mary with South Rose visible behind as seen through the open central north doors	St. Anne, Mary, details of the South rose window	North Porch, Trumeau Sculpture 1194-1230; South rose Stained glass 1221-1230
162	Biblical References Not Included in Text	Jesus with two angels incensing above him	Jesus, Angels	South Porch, Trumeau Sculpture 1194-1230
180	Before the Index	The south side of the Chartres Cathedral	View of the cathedral at dusk from the St. Chéron cemetery	Chartres, France, Department of Eure-et-Loir
BACK COVER				
BC	Back Cover	The south side of the Chartres Cathedral	View of the cathedral at dusk from the St. Chéron cemetery	Chartres, France, Department of Eure-et-Loir

PART 2: LOCATION OF IMAGES USED IN
THE UPPER CHURCH

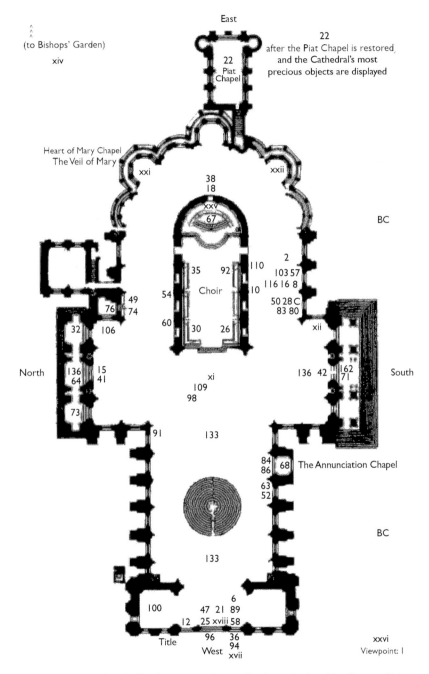

Locations are identified by the page numbers and/or letters in the table of images (2.1 above) This map of Chartres Cathedral is adapted from Marcel-Joseph Bulteau, 1850.

East

Notre-
Dame de
Sous-Terre

5
44

Statue
Our Lady
of the Crypt

78 Small piece of
the Veil of Mary
in a reliquary

104

Marie
Porte
du Ciel
Window

Notre -
Dame
de Sous-
Terre
Chapel

*

V

North

South

West

This map of Chartres Cathedral is adapted from Marcel-Joseph Bulteau, 1850.

PART 4: TABLE OF MARIAN IMAGERY
IN CHARTRES CATHEDRAL

Beginning with Yves Delaporte's list of Marys[1] in the Chartres Cathedral (1955), Alain Pierre Louët and the author compiled this table of Marian imagery, which reflects the experience of her presence in the building and parish life of the cathedral. This list is not exhaustive, but in offering it here, we hope to inspire deeper understanding as well as further research. There are many related subjects that could be undertaken, such as the study of symbols and numbers relating to Mary, including flowers, stones, and biblical typological references to her in the cathedral.

Additions to Delaporte's list are shown in bold and noted in Roman numbers. Images shown in this book are marked with an asterisk after their number. Works that no longer exist are shown in italics.

DELAPORTE'S #	DESCRIPTION OF THE IMAGE OF MARY AND ITS LOCATION	DATE
	I. HISTORY OF MARY	
	Birth of Mary **(Protoevangelium of James 5:2)**[1]	
1	Mary's first bath: (S:[2] W capital frieze, scene 5, N portal)[3]	1145[4]
2	Birth of Mary: Being presented to Anne by the midwife (SG[5]16:[6] S ambulatory)	1217–20
3	Birth of Mary: Mary's first bath (SG16: S ambulatory, Life of Mary Window)	1217–20

1 Yves Delaporte, *Les trois Notre-Dame de la cathédrale de Chartres, étude suivie de la liste des images de la Vierge appartenant à la cathédrale et de quelques mots sur le pèlerinage de Chartres* (Chartres : Houvet, 1955), 71–84.

2 S: indicates a sculpted work. Unless noted otherwise the material used was stone.

3 Many details have been added to the original list so that readers will be able to find the images more easily and understand the nature of the images more fully.

4 As much as possible specific dates have been included. They are generally taken from the University of Pittsburgh site on the Chartres Cathedral, http://images.library.pitt.edu/c /chartres/, or the French government site, http://www.culture.gouv.fr/culture/inventai /patrimoine/.

5 SG: stained-glass image.

6 In honor of Delaporte's work, his numbering system for the windows has been used.

DELAPORTE'S #	DESCRIPTION OF THE IMAGE OF MARY AND ITS LOCATION	DATE
	Birth of Mary *(Protoevangelium of James 5:2)*	
4	Birth of Mary: Mary's first bath (S: S ambulatory, outer choir scene 4[7], Jehan Soulas[8])	1519
	Young Mary in the arms, on the lap, or beside her mother Anne **(apocryphal:** *Protoevangelium of James***)**	
5*	Standing Anne holding Mary (S: N porch, central doorway, Trumeau)	1194–1220
6*	Standing Anne holds Mary: (SG 145: central lancet of N rose)	1221–30
I	**Representation of 6 (T[9] with embroidery: sacristy, priest's stole)**	**2006**
II	**Standing Anne holds young Mary by her side (S, wooden: Pillar Chapel)**	**1850–1859**
7	Mary on Anne's lap (SG 151, N crossing, west side)	1880
8	Modern window in the Chapel of St. Anne (SG crypt: damaged in 1944, has since disappeared.	19th c.
	Mary Taken to the Temple: **(apocryphal:** *The Golden Legend***)**	
9	Mary taken to the temple (S: scene 7, central portal)	1145
10	Mary mounting the steps to the temple (S: W capital frieze, 8, central portal)	1145
11	Mary climbing steps to the temple (S: S ambulatory, outer choir scene 5, Jehan Soulas)	1520–21
	Mary at School (Possibly unique at Chartres due to the presence of the School of Chartres)	
12*	Mary and parents meet the teacher at school (SG16: S ambulatory, Life of Mary)	1217–20
13*	Mary in class at school (SG16: S ambulatory, Life of Mary Window)	1217–20

7   Dates for scenes from the outer choir sculptures are taken from Françoise Jouanneaux, *Le Tour du chœur de la cathédrale de Chartres* (Orléans: Association Régionale pour l'Étude du Patrimoine de la Région Centre, 2000).

8   When an artist has been identified, she or he will be included.

9   T: Textile.

DELAPORTE'S #	DESCRIPTION OF THE IMAGE OF MARY AND ITS LOCATION	DATE
	Engagement or Marriage of Mary **(apocryphal: *Protoevangelium of James*)**	
III	**Mary presented to Joseph (W facade, capital frieze, S: scene 9, Central Portal)**	**1145**
	Mary and Joseph fold a flowering rod (M: sacristy, 2 chalices, Chertier)	**1857, 1865**
14	Marriage of Mary and Joseph (S: W capital frieze, scene 10, central portal)	1145
IV	**Joseph takes Mary home (S: W capital frieze, scene 11, central portal)**	**1145**
15	Joseph selected as husband of Mary (SG16: S ambulatory, Life of Mary)	1217–20
16	Engagement or marriage of Mary and Joseph (SG16: S ambulatory, Life of Mary)	1217–20
17	Engagement or marriage of Mary and Joseph (S: S ambulatory, outer choir scene 6, Jean Soulas)	1520–21
	The Annunciation of the Birth of Jesus **(biblical: Luke 1:26–38)**	
18	The Annunciation (S: W facade, cap Fr, S: scene 12, between cen portal & N portal)	1145
19*	The Annunciation (S: West wall: lintel of the S portal)	1145
20*	The Annunciation (SG2: west wall, Life of Christ Window, bottom row)	1145–55
V	**Representation of 20 (T with embroidery: sacristy, priest's chasuble)**	2006
21	The Annunciation (S: N porch, E bay, sculptures on columns, E side)	1194–1230
22	The Annunciation (SG16: S ambulatory, Life of Mary Window)	1217–20
23*	The Annunciation (SG120: upper apsidal window, above center of the choir)	1210–25
24	The Annunciation (SG150: N transept, W side, clerestory, Annunciation & Vis)	1230–35
25	The Annunciation (SG135: N transept, E side, clerestory, infancy of Christ)	1230–34
26	The Annunciation (S: rood screen; currently in storage)	1230–60
27	The Annunciation (S: rood screen; capstone with relief, currently in storage)	1230–60

DELAPORTE'S #	DESCRIPTION OF THE IMAGE OF MARY AND ITS LOCATION	DATE
	The Annunciation of the Birth of Jesus cont.	
28	The Annunciation (SG19: S ambulatory, grisaille, Annunciation Window)	14th c.
VI	**Representation of 28 (T with embroidery: sacristy, Mary only, priest's stole)**	**2006**
29	The Annunciation (SG Piat: 3rd window from the doorway, on the left)	1350
30	The Annunciation (S: outside of the Vendôme chapel, both sides of window)	15th or 16th c.
31	The Annunciation (S: S ambulatory, outer choir scene 7, Jehan Soulas)	1520–21
32	The Annunciation (S: S ambulatory, outer choir, to the left of the clock, embroidery on the bottom of a bishop's alb)	16th c.
33	The Annunciation (SBR[10]: S tower off narthex, west side, Pierre-Fr Berruer)	1769
VII	**The Annunciation (Ms[11]: Pontifical of Chartres, BM144, Orléans,[12] f. 81v**	Early 13th c.
VIII	**The Annunciation (Fr[13]: Caveau des Evêques)**	1364
IX	**The Annunciation (Fr: crypt, *Notre-Dame de Sous-Terre Chapel*, near Marie, Porte du Ciel window, N arm, W side)**	**Undated**
X	**The Annunciation (M[14]: gold, silver, etc., reliquary of Jesus's circumcision, sacristy)**	16th c.
XI	**The Annunciation (M: sacristy, chalice #3[15], on the base)**	1650
XII	**The Annunciation (M: gilded silver, sacristy, chalice, ref. PM28000899)**	17th c.
XIII	**The Annunciation (M: sacristy, chalice of the Marquise of Rochejaquelein by Alexandre Thierry, reference IM28000211)**	1838–45
XIV	**Chapel[16] of the Annunciation, also known as Vendôme chapel (S aisle)**	1417

10 SBR: sculpted bas-relief.
11 Ms: Manuscript.
12 Although this manuscript is no longer at Chartres, it is important because its images are very like those found in the glass and sculpture of the cathedral in the thirteenth century. F 0v includes an oath of office taken by Bishop of Chartres, Albéric Cornut (1236–43).
13 FR: fresco.
14 M: metalwork.
15 # signifies the listing on the French government site: www.palissy.fr.
16 C: chapel.

DELAPORTE'S #	DESCRIPTION OF THE IMAGE OF MARY AND ITS LOCATION	DATE
The Visitation **(biblical: Luke 1:39–56)**		
34	The Visitation (S: W facade, cap Fr, S: scene 13, between cen portal & N portal)	1145
35*	The Visitation (S: W wall: lintel of S doorway)	1145
36	The Visitation (SG2: west wall, central window, Life of Christ, bottom, center)	1145–55
XV	**Representation of 36 (T with embroidery: sacristy, priest's chasuble)**	**2006**
XVI	**Representation of 36 (T with embroidery: sacristy, priest's stole)**	**2006**
37	The Visitation (S: N porch, 2 figures on the right side of the E doorway)	1194–1220
38	The Visitation (SG16: S ambulatory, Life of Mary Window)	1217–20
39	The Visitation (SG120: upper apsidal window, above the center of the choir)	1210–25
40	The Visitation (SG150: N transept, W side, clerestory, Annunciation & Visitation)	1230–35
41	The Visitation (S: S ambulatory, outer choir scene 8, Jehan Soulas)	1521–35
XVII	**The Visitation (P[17]: Vendôme chapel, S aisle)**	**1676**
Mary sewing, during Joseph's dream **(biblical base: Matthew 1:18–25)**		
42	Joseph dreaming, Mary sewing (S: S ambulatory, outer choir scene 9, Jehan Soulas)	1521–1535
The Birth of Jesus/The Nativity of Jesus **(biblical: Luke 2:1–7)**		
43	The Nativity (S: W capital frieze, scene 14, N portal, S side)	1145
44	The Nativity (S: west wall: lintel of S doorway)	1145
45*	The Nativity (SG2: west wall, central window, Life of Christ, bottom row, right)	1145–55
XVIII	**Representation of 45 (T with embroidery: sacristy, priest's chasuble)**	**2006**
XIX	**Representation of 45 (T with embroidery: sacristy, priest's stole)**	**2006**

17   P: painting.

DELAPORTE'S #	DESCRIPTION OF THE IMAGE OF MARY AND ITS LOCATION	DATE
	The Birth of Jesus/The Nativity of Jesus cont.	
XX	**The Nativity (Ms: Pontifical of Chartres, BM144, Orléans, f. 77v)**	**Early 13th c.**
46	The Nativity (S: N porch, lintel over the E doorway)	1194–1220
47	The Nativity (SG16: S ambulatory, Life of Mary Window)	1217–20
48	The Nativity (SG105: choir clerestory, S side, Nativity & Flight to Egypt)	1210–25
49	The Nativity (SG136: upper window, N transept, E side next to the crossing)	1230–35
50*	The Nativity (S: rood screen; currently in storage)	1230–60
51	The Nativity (PM:[18] crypt, S gallery, above S area for water used at Mass)	13th c.
52*	The Nativity (S: S ambulatory, outer choir scene 10, Jehan Soulas)	1521–35
XXI	**The Nativity (M: gilded silver, sacristy, chalice, ref. PM28000899)**	**17th c.**
	Other modern images of the Nativity appear from time to time in the cathedral, including images on votive candles during Advent and Christmas as well as the pieces of the modern cathedral crèche.	**20th-21st c.**
**	**Related to the Annunciation and the Nativity is the cathedral relic of the veil (numerous pieces found in the Veil Chapel, crypt, sacristy, and the diocesan archives) and symbolic representations of it. There are more than 100 other images of the "little shirt" in wood, stone, glass, precious metals, fabric, and other materials.[19]**	**1st–21st c.**
	The Shepherd's Visit to the Holy Family (biblical: Luke 2:8–19)	
53	The shepherds' visit (SBR: inner choir, N side, nearest crossing, Bridan)	1786–88
	The Wise Men from the East Visit Jesus and Mary (biblical: Matthew 2:1-12)	
54	Visit of Wise Men (S: W capital frieze, N portal, S side, scene 18)	1145
55*	Visit of Wise Men (SG2: west wall, central window)	1145–55

18   PM: Mural painting.

19   While visually referencing the veil, it also continues to be used by the cathedral chapter as their chosen symbol. For example, on various doors and around the choir there are twelve symbolic shirts that represent the veil, but also the power and authority of the priests who conducted services throughout the day in this area.

DELAPORTE'S #	DESCRIPTION OF THE IMAGE OF MARY AND ITS LOCATION	DATE
56*	Visit of Wise Men (S: N porch, E bay, sculptures on lintel, E side)	1194–1220
57	Visit of Wise Men (SG106: upper choir, S side, second window from crossing)	1210–25
58*	Visit of Wise Men (SG16: S ambulatory, Life of Mary window)	1217–20
59	Visit of Wise Men (SG136: upper wind., N transept, E side next to the crossing)	1230–35
60	Visit of Wise Men (S: rood screen; currently in storage)	1230–60
61*	Visit of Wise Men (S: S ambulatory, outer choir scene 12, Jehan Soulas)	1521–35
62	Visit of Wise Men (SBR: inner choir, S side, closest to crossing, Bridan)	1786–88
XXII	**Visit of the Wise Men (M: Sacristy, chalice, Poussielgue-Rusand)**	1877

The Circumcision of Jesus
(biblical: Luke 2:21)

63	The Circumcision of Jesus (S: S ambulatory, outer choir scene 11, Jehan Soulas)	1521–35

The Presentation of Jesus at the Temple
(biblical: Luke 2:22-39)

XXIII	**Presentation (S: W capital frieze, central portal, N side, scene 22)**	**1145**
64	Presentation (S: west wall: lintel of S doorway)	1145
65*	Presentation (SG2: west wall)	1145–55
XXIV	**Presentation (Ms: Pontifical of Chartres, BM144, Orléans, f. 81)**	**Early 13th c.**
66*	Presentation (SG16: S ambulatory, Life of Mary window)	1217–20
67	Presentation (SG152: clerestory, N transept, W side, second window from crossing, Announcement to the Shepherds and Presentation Window)	1225–33
68	Presentation (S: rood screen; currently in storage)	1230–60
69	*Presentation (S: S ambulatory, outer choir scene 13, F Marchand). The statue of Mary no longer exists.*	*1542–43*
70	Presentation (SBR: inner choir, N side, center image, Bridan)	1786–88

DELAPORTE'S #	DESCRIPTION OF THE IMAGE OF MARY AND ITS LOCATION	DATE
	The Flight to Egypt **(biblical: Matthew 2:13–15)**	
71	Flight to Egypt (S:W capital frieze, N portal, N side, scene 19)	1145
72	Flight to Egypt (SG2: west wall, Life of Christ Window, 5th row from top, left)	1145–55
73*	Flight to Egypt (SG16: S ambulatory, Life of Mary Window)	1217–20
74	Flight to Egypt (SG4: S aisle, first window from W, St. John the Evangelist wind.)	1205–15
75*	Flight to Egypt (SG105: choir clerestory, S side, Nativity & Flight to Egypt Window)	1210–25
76	Flight to Egypt (SBF: outer choir, behind Massacre of Innocents, F Marchand	1542–44
77	Return to Egypt (SG2: west wall, Life of Christ window)	1145
	Mary finding Jesus in the Temple **(biblical: Luke 2:41–51)**	
78	Mary, Joseph, Jesus (SBR: outer choir behind the Baptism of Christ)	16th c.
79*	Mary Speaks to Jesus, Cana (SG14, lower: S ambulatory, Our Lady of the Beautiful Window)	1215–20
80*	Mary with Servants, Cana (SG14, lower: S ambulatory)	1215–20
XXV	**Wedding of Cana (P: sacristy, inverted copy of P by Charles Poerson)**	**17th c.**
	Mary encountering Jesus who was Carrying his Cross **(devotional practices: Stations of the Cross)**	
81	Mary, encounters Jesus with his cross (SBR: S aisle, station 8, Saupique)	1941–49
	Mary at the Foot of the Cross **(biblical: John 19:25)**	
82*	Mary near cross (SG3: west wall, S window, Passion & Resurrection)	1145–55
83	Mary near cross (SG59: North aisle, next to crossing, Typological Passion)	1876
84*	Mary near cross (SG18: S ambulatory, small rose, Christ on the Cross)	ca. 1220

DELAPORTE'S #	DESCRIPTION OF THE IMAGE OF MARY AND ITS LOCATION	DATE
XXVI	**Mary near cross (W²⁰&M: copper, gold, enamel, sacristy, tabernacle, Limousin)**	**Early 13th c.**
85	Mary near Cross (SG Piat: 2nd window from the doorway, on the right)	1350
86	Mary near cross (SG8: S aisle, Vendôme chapel)	after 1413
XXVII	**Mary near cross (M: gold leaf, copper, enamel, sacristy)**	**16th c.**
XXVIII	**Mary near Cross (M: sacristy, chalice of the Marquise of Rochejaquelein Alexandre Thierry, reference IM28000211)**	**1838–45**
87	Mary near cross (SBR: S aisle, station 12, Mary, Saupique)	1941-49
XXIX	**Mary near cross (M: silver, gold, sacristy, chalice #10)**	**1847**
XXX	**Mary near cross (M: silver, gold, copper, enamel, sacristy, chalice #5)**	**ca. 1903**
XXXI	**Mary near cross (M: silver, gold, copper, enamel, sacristy, Paten #5, P Brunet)**	**1903**
XXXII	**Mary near cross (M: location unknown, belonged to Chanoine Manuel)**	**Unknown**
	### Mary Fainting by the Cross **(Apocryphal Gospel of Nicodemus, also called the Acts of Pilate)**	
88	Mary, fainting as the cross is put up (S: outer choir, N ambulatory, scene 27, Mazière)	1714
	### Mary present at the Descent of Jesus from the Cross **(narratives from the Middle Ages, extrabiblical)**	
89*	Mary at descent (SG3: west wall, S window, Passion & Resurrection window)	1145–55
XXXIII	**Mary at descent (Ms: Pontifical of Chartres, BM144, Orléans, f. 70)**	**Early 13th c.**
XXXIV	**Mary at descent (M: silver, gold, Sacristy, Paten, A. Thierry A)**	**1823**
XXXV	**Mary at descent (SG59: North aisle, next to crossing, typological Passion)**	**1876**
XXXVI	**Mary at descent (SBR: S aisle, station 13, Saupique)**	**1941–49**

20   W: wood.

DELAPORTE'S #	DESCRIPTION OF THE IMAGE OF MARY AND ITS LOCATION	DATE
Mary mourning her dead Son, Jesus: Pietà **(extrabiblical, developed in the Middle Ages, one of the** **3 expressions of a sorrowful Mary (the other two** **are *Mater Dolorosa* and *Stabat Mater*)**		
90	Pietà (S: S ambulatory, outer choir, to the left of the clock, small detail on the clasp of a cape worn by a bishop)	16th c.
91	Pietà (S: N ambulatory, outer choir, scene 28, Simon Mazière)	1714
92	Pietà (SBR: inner choir, S side, central image, Bridan)	1786–88
XXXVII	**Pietà (F: sacristy, liturgical cape, beige silk with gold thread, embroidered)**	18th–19th c.
XXXVIII	**Pietà (M: sacristy, ciborium, Hippolyte François Bertrand-Paraud)**	1837
XXXIX	**Pietà (T: sacristy, liturgical cape)**	Unknown
Mary present at the burial of Jesus' body **(extrabiblical, may have grown out of liturgical drama)**		
XL*	**Mary at Jesus's burial (SG3: west wall, S window, Passion & Resurrection)**	1145–55
XLI	**Mary at Jesus's burial (SG59: North aisle, next to crossing, Passion)**	1205–15
93	Mary at Jesus's burial (SBR: S aisle, station 14, Saupique)	1941–49
Mary Present at Jesus's Empty Tomb **(extrabiblical, highly unusual image)**		
XLII*	**Mary at tomb with Angel & 2 women (SG3: west wall, S window)**	1145–55
Jesus appearance to Mary after his resurrection **(extrabiblical: *The Golden Legend*)**		
94	Jesus appears to Mary and John (S: N ambulatory, outer choir, scene 33)	ca. 1516
95*	Mary at Jesus's ascension (S: N ambulatory, outer choir, scene 34)	ca. 1516
Mary Praying for Pentecost with the Apostles **(biblical: Acts 1:12–14)**		
96*	Mary with apostles praying (S: N ambulatory, outer choir, scene 35)	ca. 1516

DELAPORTE'S #	DESCRIPTION OF THE IMAGE OF MARY AND ITS LOCATION	DATE
Mary present at Pentecost **(possibly biblical—no one mentioned by name Acts 2:1–4)**		
XLIII	**Mary, Pentecost (Ms: Pontifical of Chartres, BM144, Orléans, f. 92v)**	**Early 13th c.**
Mary venerating the Cross **(extrabiblical: *The Golden Legend*, *The Exaltation of the Holy Cross*)**		
97	Mary venerating the cross (S: N ambulatory, outer choir, scene 36)	ca. 1516
The death of Mary **(extrabiblical: *The Golden Legend*)**		
98	The death of Mary (S: N Porch, central doorway, lintel)	1194–1220
99*	The death of Mary (SG7: S aisle, 4th window from W; Death and Glorification of Mary)	1205–15
XLIV	**Death of Mary (Ms: Pontifical of Chartres, BM144, Orléans, f. 94)**	**Early 13th c.**
100	The death of Mary (SG153: Clerestory, N Transept, W, next to the crossing)	1225–33
101	The death of Mary (S: N ambulatory, outer choir, scene 37)	ca. 1516
XLV	**Assumption of Mary (P: crypt ceiling, NDdST chapel, Delaronce, Pauvert, Verpré)**	**1645**
XLVI	The death of Mary (P: Vendôme Chapel: S aisle, Jean François Bosio)	1819
Mary's body carried to her tomb **(extrabiblical: *The Golden Legend*)**		
102	Mary's body carried to her tomb (SG7: S aisle, Death and Glorification of Mary)	1205–15
XLVII	**Mary's body carried to tomb (S: N ambulatory, outer choir, scene 38)**	**ca. 1516**
103	Mary's body placed in the tomb (SG7: S aisle, Death and Glorificat. Mary)	1205–15
Mary's soul received by Jesus **(extrabiblical)**		
XLVIII	**Jesus receives Mary's soul (SG7: S aisle Death and Glorification of Mary)**	**1205–15**

DELAPORTE'S #	DESCRIPTION OF THE IMAGE OF MARY AND ITS LOCATION	DATE
	The Resurrection of Mary **(extrabiblical; church tradition)**	
104*	Resurrection of Mary (S: N porch, central doorway, lintel)	1194–1220
105	The resurrection of Mary (S: N ambulatory, outer choir, scene 39)	ca. 1516
	The Assumption of Mary into Heaven **(extrabiblical; church tradition)**	
106*	Assumption of Mary (SG7: S aisle, Death and Glorification of Mary)	1205–15
XLIX	**Representation of 106 (T with embroidery: sacristy, priest's stole)**	**2006**
L	**Assumption, Mary (Ms: Pontifical of Char, BM144, Orléans, f. 94)**	**Early 13th c.**
107	Assumption, Mary (SG153: Clerestory, N Transept, W, next to crossing)	1225–33
LI	**Assumption of Mary (P: crypt ceiling, NDdST chapel, Delaronce, Pauvert, Verpré)**	**1645**
LII	**Assumption of Mary (M: sacristy, chalice #3, ref. IM28000209)**	**ca. 1650**
108*	Assumption of Mary (S: marble, above the high altar in the choir, Bridan)	1773
	The crowning of Mary in Heaven **(extrabiblical; church tradition)**	
109	Coronation of Mary (S: N porch, central doorway, tympanum)	1194–1220
110	Jesus crowns Mary (SG7: S aisle, death and glorification of Mary)	1205–15
111	Coronation of Mary (SG153: clerestory, N transept, W, next to crossing)	1225–33
112*	Coronation of Mary (SG8: S aisle, Vendôme chapel)	after 1413
113	Coronation of Mary (S: N ambulatory, outer choir, scene 40)	ca. 1516

DELAPORTE'S #	DESCRIPTION OF THE IMAGE OF MARY AND ITS LOCATION	DATE
	II NONHISTORICAL IMAGES OF MARY	
	Mary, sitting with her young son, Jesus	
114*	Mary Throne, incensing angels on side (S: West wall: lintel of the S portal)	1145
115*	Our Lady of the Beautiful Window (SG14: S ambulatory N-D Belle Verrière)	1180
LIII	**Representation of 116 (T with embroidery: sacristy, priest's stole)**	**2006**
116*	Mary Throne (SG2: west wall, central window, Life of Christ, top)	1145–55
117	Mary Throne (SG9: S aisle, 6th window, Miracles of Mary)	1928
118*	Seated Mary with standing Jesus blessing (SG26, S ambulatory, donor Marguerite prays)	1220–27
119	Seated Mary with Jesus blessing priest-donor (SG28, SE ambulatory)	1220–25
120	Seated Mary with Jesus blessing priest-donor (SG35, E ambulatory)	1220–25
121	Seated Mary with standing Jesus blessing deacon-donor (SG40, NE ambulatory)	1220–25
122	Seated Mary with standing Jesus blessing priest-donor (SG54, N ambulatory, Pillar Chapel)	1225–35
123*	Mary Throne, Jesus blessing, donors on side (SG157; clerestory N nave)	1210–25
124*	Mary Throne, Jesus blessing, HS descends (SG134, N choir next to crossing)	1217
125*	Mary Throne, Jesus blessing (SG120; Upper choir E, top of apsidal wind.)	1220–25
LIV	**Representation of 125 (T with embroidery: sacristy, priest's stole)**	**2006**
126*	Seated Mary with Jesus blessing (SG101, clerestory rose, S transept, E side)	1225–30
127	Mary Throne, Jesus stands and blesses (SG98, clerestory rose, S trans, E side)	1225–30
128*	Seated Mary with Jesus blessing (SG145, center of N rose)	1235
LV	**Representation of 128 (T with embroidery: sacristy, priest's chasuble)**	**2006**
129	Seated Mary, Jesus blessing (S: S Porch, central doorway gable)	1194–1220

DELAPORTE'S #	DESCRIPTION OF THE IMAGE OF MARY AND ITS LOCATION	DATE
	Nonhistorical Images of Mary cont.	
130	Mary Throne, Jesus blessing (S: rood screen; capstone, currently in storage)	1230–60
131	Seated Mary, Jesus on right side of lap (SG Piat: NW window)	1350
LVI	**Seated Mary with Jesus on right side (P on limestone retable: crypt)**	**16th c.**
132*	Mary Throne, Jesus blesses (S: N ambulatory, Our Lady of the Pillar) *Notre-Dame du Pilier* (NDdP)	1508
LVII	**Representation NDdP 132 (E[21]: Sacristy, Larmessin)**	**1697**
LVIII	**Representation NDdP 132 (M: chalice #1, Sacristy, A Gueyton)**	**1885**
LIX	**Representation NDdP 132 (W: Prie-Dieu of Cardinal Pie)**	**1849**
LX	**Representation NDdP 132 on chalice # 8 (M: Sacristy, M Thierry)**	**1853–55**
133*	Young Mary with playful Jesus on lap (M: Bronze, relief, base of the cross on the top of the N tower)	1692
134*	Mary Throne, Jesus blesses (SW: Crypt, N, *Notre-Dame de Sous-Terre*/Our Lady of the Crypt)	1976
135	Mary Throne imitate NDdST 134 (PM: crypt, St. Yves Chapel, *Regina Angelorum*)	19th c.
136	Mary Throne imitate NDdST 134 (PM: St Yves Chap, *Regina Virginum*)	19th c.
LXI	**Representation NDdST 134 (M: chalice #1, sacristy, A. Gueyton)**	**1885**
LXII	Representation NDdST 134 (T: sacristy, white chasuble, "Go to the altar of God")	**1844, 1894**
LXIII	**Representation NDdST 134 on chalice # 8 (M: Sacristy, M Thierry)**	**1853–55**
LXIV	**Representation 134 (M: storage, sign, *Virgini Pariturae*)**	**1856**
LXV	**Representation NDdST 134 (W: storage, sign, Isaiah)**	**1857**
LXVI	**Representation NDdST 134 (M: sacristy, chalice #12, Brunet)**	**1871**
LXVII	**Representation NDdST 134 (M: sacristy, chalice, Chertier)**	**1873**
LXVIII	**Representation NDdST 134 (M: bishop's staff, Poussielgue-Rusand)**	**1876**

21   E: etching.

DELAPORTE'S #	DESCRIPTION OF THE IMAGE OF MARY AND ITS LOCATION	DATE
LXIX	**Representation NDdST 134 (EN:Veil Chapel, Veil Reliquary)**	1876
LXX	**Representation NDdST 134 (M: bishop's seal of Mgr. Harscouët)**	ca. 1940
LXXI	**Representation NDdST 134 (M: sacristy, chalice, Demarquet)**	1886
LXXII	**Representation NDdST 134 (M: sacristy, front cover of canon)**	1895
LXXIII	**Representation NDdST 134 (T: sacristy, white with yellow interior)**	Unknown
137	Seated Mary, Jesus holding her (SG12: S trans. lower, François Lorin)	1954
LXXIV	**Seated Mary, Jesus on lap (T: sacristy, chasuble, red with gold)**	Unknown
LXXV	**Seated Mary, Jesus sits frontally (T: sacristy, chasuble, white)**	Unknown
138	Mary offering to nurse Jesus (SG71: clerestory, S nave, 5th window)	1205–15
139*	Mary offering to nurse Jesus (SG15: S ambulatory, small upper rose)	1215–20
LXXVI	**Representation of 139 (T with embroidery: sacristy, priest's stole)**	2006
140*	Mary stands holding Jesus (SG: lancet SG95: S transept, under rose)	1221–30
141	Mary stands holding Jesus (S: sprocket above S porch)	14th c.
142	Mary stands holding Jesus (SG: sprocket above N porch)	14th c.
143	Mary holds Jesus & his foot (SG10: grisaille, S transept, W side)	14th c.
144	Mary holds Jesus near her shoulder (S: SE ambulatory, above door to Piat Chap)	14th c.
LXXVII	**Exact copy of 144 (S: Piat Chapel, above the entrance doors, top of stairs)**	Unknown
LXXVIII	**Copy of 144 (bishop's residence)**	Unknown
145	Mary holds Jesus, they exchange looks (SG: Piat Chapel, SE window)	1350
146	Mary (no head) stands with Jesus (WS:[22] S ambulatory on a door to an inner chapel	16th c.
147	Mary stands with Jesus (WS: S nave in the center of the grand organ)	16th c.

22   WS: wooden statue.

DELAPORTE'S #	DESCRIPTION OF THE IMAGE OF MARY AND ITS LOCATION	DATE
	Images Representing Statues cont.	
CV	**Representation of NDdST 134 (SW: cathedral, small copy of earlier statue)**	20th c.
CVI	**Representation of NDdST 134 (M: sacristy, liturgical crosses worn by priests with Mary's tunic the sign of the chapter on the back)**	20th c.
CVII	**King Charles offers the veil to Mary and Jesus, veil reliquary (EN: Veil Chapel)**	1876
CVIII	**Mary seated, Jesus on left knee (M: Sacristy, T, chasuble, white silk, gold disks)**	1894
CIX	Seated Mary (frontal), Jesus facing left (M: Sacristy, chalice #17, 3 parts)	1913
CX	**Seated Mary with Jesus on left knee (T: Sacristy, Chasuble, white with gold trim)**	20th c.
160*	Mary in the tree of Jesse, [MA 24] Jesus above (SG1, 2nd from top)	1145
CXI	**Mary Throne (T: Crypt, North Gallery, S Wall, NDdST chapel)**	1200
161	Mary, the gifts of the Spirit (SG166: clerestory, N nave, Jesus inside Mary)	1205–15
CXII	**Mary and Jesus (PM: Caveau des Évêques, top of E wall)**	1364
CXIII	**Mary on the right of Jesus (M: Sacristy, processional cross)**	16th c.
CXIV	**Mary and Jesus in a cloud saving a shipwrecked man (PW,[25] oil, sacristy)**	17th c.
CXV	**Mary and Jesus in a cloud, king and queen of England kneeling (PW, oil, Sacristy)**	17th c.
CXVI	**Mary spins, Joseph works, Jesus rakes (P: oil, sacristy)**	18th c.
CXVII	**Mary holds Jesus (M: sacristy, ciborium, J Jamain & E Chevron)**	1865
CXVIII*	**Mary, Doorway to Heaven (SG, crypt, N arm of Pillar Chapel)**	21rst
162	Mary,[MA] seated with an open book (S: W Sprocket of South porch)	1194–1230
163	Mary, Legend of Theophilus 1 (SG9: S aisle, Miracles of Mary)	1927
164*	Mary, Legend of Theophilus 2 (SG9; S aisle, Miracles of Mary)	1927

24   MA: Images in which Mary appears alone
25   PW: painting on wood.

DELAPORTE'S #	DESCRIPTION OF THE IMAGE OF MARY AND ITS LOCATION	DATE
165*	Mary, Intercessor at Last Judgment (S: S porch, central doorway, tympanum)	1194–1230
166	Mary, Intercessor at Last Judgment (SG: Piat Chapel, central window)	1350
167	Mary, Intercessor at Last Judgment (SG8: S aisle, Vendôme chapel)	after 1431
168*	Mary sits with Jesus (SBR: SE inner choir, Louis XIII's vow, Bridan)	1786–88
169	Mary protects cathedral in fire of 1836[MA] (WBR:[26] crypt, Pyanet Victor)	1839
170	*Mary prays with infant Jesus (SG: Crypt, St. Nicholas chapel) Disappeared.*	19th c.
171	The Immaculate Conception[MA] (SG: crypt, Chapel of Mary Magdalene)	1860–61
172	*Mary, "of St. Luke" (P: crypt at the bottom of the south stairs) Disappeared.*	19th c.
173	Mary offering to nurse Jesus (SG: Piat, NW window)	20th c.
174	Mary with folded hands praying[MA] (SG: Piat Chapel, NW window)	20th c.
175*	Mary, healing Bishop Fulbert (SG12: S trans. lower, François Lorin)	1954

OTHER IMAGES OF MARY BY HERSELF

CXIX	**Mary, possibly pregnant[MA] (S: Above lower doorway to cathedral from Piat chapel)**	**16th c.**
CXX	**Our Lady of the Veil Icon[MA] (WP: Ecumenical Chapel)**	**18th c.**
CXXI **CXXII**	**Mary's Face[MA] (M: Sacristy, burettes-2, Alexandre Thierry, reference IM28000211)**	**1838**
CXXIII	**Mary, standing with open arms[MA] (M: sacristy, chalice, gilded silver, Alexandre Thierry Ref. PM28000743)**	**1838–45**
CXXIV	**Mary with arms crossed (M: silver, gold, enamel, chalice)**	**1862**
CXXV	**Profile of Mary (sacristy, ciborium #6, Marie Thierry)**	**1856**
CXXVI	**Crowned Mary with prayer hands, wearing veil (M: sacristy gilded silver, enamel chalice, Abbé Brimont, P Poussielgue-Rusand)**	**1885**
CXXVII	**Crowned Mary with arm crossed over chest (T: sacristy, stole)**	**20th c.**

26   WBR: wooden bas-relief.

DELAPORTE'S #	DESCRIPTION OF THE IMAGE OF MARY AND ITS LOCATION	DATE
	Other Images of Mary by Herself cont.	
CXXVIII	**Mary Standing, holding book (P: NE ambulatory, Heart of Mary Chapel, inside letter C, calligraphy sign for the Veil of Mary)**	20th c.
CXXIX	**Our Lady of the Veil Icon (WP: Chapel of Sacred Heart of Mary)**	20th c.
CXXX	**Crowned Mary with inscription, "Immaculate Mary, pray for us" (T: Sacristy, cover for communion cup)**	20th c.
CXXXI	**Mary, crowned, pointing to her sacred heart (T: Stole of Mgr. Harscouët)**	20th c.
CXXXII	**Mary, standing on a cloud (T: Cathedral Storage, Blue Banner)**	20th c.
CXXXIII	**Our Lady of the Veil Icon (WP: Cathedral)**	21st c.
CXXXIV	**Mary with folded hands (M: Sacristy, chalice with blue ovals)**	Unknown
CXXXV	**Mary, Queen of the Angels (M: Sacristy, tray for burettes)**	Unknown
CXXXVI	**Mary with halo (M, sacristy, 2 large candlesticks with claw feet)**	Unknown
	RELATED TO MARY IN THE CATHEDRAL	
	Bell with the baptismal name of Mary (N Bell Tower, heaviest bell: "Gros" Bourdon, Bell #1)	1840
	C: Chapel of the Heart of Mary (NE ambulatory, Location of the Veil, also known as the Chapel of the Martyrs)	

GLOSSARY

Annunciation The announcement of the Incarnation by the angel Gabriel to Mary (Luke 1:26–38).

Assumption of Mary The taking of Mary's body and soul to heaven. Most Catholics believe that this happened after her death. All images at Chartres reflect this. The assumption of Mary became a dogma of the Catholic Church in 1950, but the belief in her assumption was already held in the Middle Ages when Chartres Cathedral was built. It is celebrated by the Catholic, Orthodox, and parts of the Anglican churches on August 15.

Baroque A period from the late sixteenth century through the mid-eighteenth century during which an emotional artistic style that used exaggerated lighting flourished.

Bétaire Died 623. Also known as Bohaire and Boetharius. An early bishop of Chartres. In the *Vita Betharii Eposcopi Carnotensil* an early reference to Mary at Chartres is included. "One day when the blessed Bishop Betharius lay before the altar of the Ever-Virginal Mary, completely prostrate" (13).

Bernard of Chartres Born unknown, died after 1124. The chancellor (head) at the School of Chartres from 1115 until at least 1124. He was a French Neoplatonist philosopher.

Bernard of Clairvaux 1090/1091–1153. French abbot who is known for his reforming efforts within the Cistercian order, and influenced the founding of sixty-eight monasteries in Western

Europe. He was an influential theologian whose emphasis on Mary had a significant impact on the Catholic Church.

canon A priest appointed by a bishop to perform various ecclesiastical functions in the diocese. A group of canons is called the cathedral chapter.

Epiphany A church feast day that celebrates the manifestation of God in Christ to the Gentiles, who are represented by the Wise Men from the East in Matthew 2:1–12. It is celebrated on January 6, twelve days after Christmas. Many in the Eastern churches call this feast the Theophany. Among Western churches it is also referred to as the Feast of the Three Kings.

feast days of Mary Four annual feast days of Mary were celebrated in Chartres, both in the cathedral with special liturgies, and in the town where fairs attracted merchants from across Europe who came to sell their products and buy others. These took place on the following dates: February 2: the Purification of Mary (after Jesus's birth); March 25: the Annunciation (angel Gabriel's meeting with Mary); August 15: the Assumption of Mary (into heaven); September 8: the Nativity (birth) of Mary.

Fulbert (d.1028) Beloved teacher at the School of Chartres and bishop of Chartres from 1006 to 1028. He is best known for rebuilding the cathedral and emphasizing the Feast of the Nativity of Mary on September 8.

fresco A mural painting that is applied to a wet lime-plastered wall. The water and pigments set in the lime, and when dry have become a part of the wall itself.

Gilbert of Poitiers 1076–1154. Twelfth-century theologian and metaphysician. He was best known for his scriptural and Boethian commentaries.

John of Salisbury 1120/1125–1180. English author, teacher, and diplomat. He was deeply influenced by Thomas Becket (1118–1170). He is best known for the *Metalogicon* (below). He became bishop of Chartres in 1176.

liturgy Literally, the "work of the people": the form and elements that are a part of services of worship.

mandorla The Italian word for almond; a shape that looks almond-like. When two circles with the same radius intersect so that the center of each lies on the circumference of the other, the shape of the area where they overlap is called a mandorla or a *vesica piscis* (bladder of the fish). The shape represents a sacred passageway. It was used in Romanesque art (such as the central west tympanum at Chartres) to surround Christ, who made the passage from heaven to earth and earth to heaven.

Mediatrix Used since the fifth century, this title for Mary refers to her role as one who intercedes on behalf of the church and individuals. It is assumed that Jesus's close relationship with his mother will make her ability to communicate others' needs to him efficacious. Bernard of Clairvaux (above) often used this name for Mary.

Metalogicon A twelfth-century defense of the verbal and logical arts of the Trivium. Also, a book written by John of Salisbury (above) in 1159. It was addressed to his mentor Thomas Becket, the archbishop of Canterbury, for whom he later served as secretary. In it he discusses and defends three of the liberal arts (trivium: grammar, rhetoric, and logic).

Middle Ages   The period between antiquity and "modernity"; beginning with the fall of the Roman Empire (fifth century) and ending with the Renaissance (fifteenth century).

Nativity The birth of Jesus Christ.

nimbus Halo or circular shape around a head to indicate holiness.

Quadrivium   Four of the seven liberal arts that were taught at the School of Chartres: These were taught after the trivium (below) and were the mathematic arts: arithmetic, geometry, music, and astronomy.

Queen Mother   The widow of a king and mother of the sovereign. Mary's case is an exception; she is only the mother of the Sovereign since God is Jesus's Father (neither Mary's husband, nor deceased).

Presentation The event described in Luke 2:22–40. According to the Gospel, Mary and Joseph took the infant Jesus to the temple in Jerusalem forty days (inclusive) after his birth to complete Mary's ritual purification after childbirth, and to perform the redemption of the firstborn son, in obedience to the Torah (Leviticus 12; Exodus 13:12–15; etc.).

Sedes Sapientiae Throne of Wisdom, a Latin devotional title for Mary.

Theotokos The God-Bearer, also translated into English as Mother of God.

Thierry of Chartres   1100–1150/1155. He followed Gilbert of Poitiers as the chancellor (head) of the School of Chartres. He is best known for two of his works, the *Hexaemeron* (relating to Genesis) and *Heptateuch* (an encyclopedia that related to the liberal arts).

tonsure A partially shaved head with short hair on the sides but left bare on top. It is worn by monks or priests. The image of Christ with a tonsure in the uppermost image of the eastern window is highly unusual.

Trivium Three of the liberal arts that were taught at the School of Chartres: grammar, rhetoric, and logic.

veneration From the Latin *venerare*, which is translated regarding with reverence or respect. The word is often applied in the Catholic context to the honoring of people who have been identified as particularly holy, such as saints. Catholics make a distinction between the veneration (of holy people such as Mary) and worship, which is always reserved uniquely for God.

Virgini pariturae Latin for the Virgin who will give birth. This title has often been associated with the statue of *Notre-Dame de Sous-Terre* in the crypt.

Visitation The visit of Mary with Elizabeth as recorded in Luke 1:39–56.

votive candle A candle used to symbolize one's prayer.

William of Conques 1090–d. after 1045. French scholastic philosopher and a noted grammarian. It is likely he wrote *De philosophia mundi* (Philosophy of the world) and *Dragmaticon*. He also wrote glosses (notes expanding the meaning of a text) on Plato's *Timaeus* and Boethius's *Consolation of Philosophy*.

BIBLICAL REFERENCES NOT INCLUDED IN THE TEXT

Listed in order by the chapter in which each appears. All biblical references cited are from the New Revised Standard Version.

Preface

LUKE 1:39–56

(Full reference of the Visitation story. The Magnificat begins after "And Mary said" and ends with "to his descendants forever."

In those days Mary set out and went with haste to a Judean town in the hill country, where she entered the house of Zechariah and greeted Elizabeth. When Elizabeth heard Mary's greeting, the child leaped in her womb. And Elizabeth was filled with the Holy Spirit and exclaimed with a loud cry, "Blessed are you among women, and blessed is the fruit of your womb. And why has this happened to me, that the mother of my Lord comes to me? For as soon as I heard the sound of your greeting, the child in my womb leaped for joy. And blessed is she who believed that there would be a fulfillment of what was spoken to her by the Lord."

And Mary said,

> "My soul magnifies the Lord,
> and my spirit rejoices in God my Savior,
> for he has looked with favor on the lowliness of his servant.
> Surely, from now on all generations will call me blessed;
> for the Mighty One has done great things for me,
> and holy is his name.
> His mercy is for those who fear him
> from generation to generation.

He has shown strength with his arm;
> he has scattered the proud in the thoughts of their hearts.

He has brought down the powerful from their thrones,
> and lifted up the lowly;

he has filled the hungry with good things,
> and sent the rich away empty.

He has helped his servant Israel,
> in remembrance of his mercy,

according to the promise he made to our ancestors,
> to Abraham and to his descendants forever."

And Mary remained with her about three months and then returned to her home.

Chapter One
MARY, MOTHER OF JESUS

1.1 Introduction

ACTS 1:13–14

When [the apostles] had entered the city, they went to the room upstairs where they were staying, Peter, and John, and James, and Andrew, Philip and Thomas, Bartholomew and Matthew, James son of Alphaeus, and Simon the Zealot, and Judas son of James. All these were constantly devoting themselves to prayer, together with certain women, including Mary the mother of Jesus, as well as his brothers.

LUKE 1:26–38

In the sixth month the angel Gabriel was sent by God to a town in Galilee called Nazareth, to a virgin engaged to a man whose name was Joseph, of the house of David. The virgin's name was Mary. And he came to her and said, "Greetings, favored one! The Lord is with you."

But she was much perplexed by his words and pondered what sort of greeting this might be. The angel said to her, "Do not be afraid, Mary, for you have found favor with God. And now, you will conceive in your womb and bear a son, and you will name him Jesus. He will be great, and will be called the Son of the Most High, and the Lord God will give to him the throne of his ancestor David. He will reign over the house of Jacob forever, and of his kingdom there will be no end." Mary said to the angel, "How can this be, since I am a virgin?" The angel said to her, "The Holy Spirit will come upon you, and the power of the Most High will overshadow you; therefore the child to be born will be holy; he will be called Son of God. And now, your relative Elizabeth in her old age has also conceived a son; and this is the sixth month for her who was said to be barren. For nothing will be impossible with God." Then Mary said, "Here am I, the servant of the Lord; let it be with me according to your word." Then the angel departed from her.

LUKE 1:39–56

See page 163

MATTHEW 1:16

Jacob the father of Joseph the husband of Mary, of whom Jesus was born, who is called the Messiah.

MATTHEW 1:18–25

Now the birth of Jesus the Messiah took place in this way. When his mother Mary had been engaged to Joseph, but before they lived together, she was found to be with child from the Holy Spirit. Her husband Joseph, being a righteous man and unwilling to expose her to public disgrace, planned to dismiss her quietly. But just when he had resolved to do this, an angel of the Lord appeared to him in a dream and said, "Joseph, son of David, do not be afraid to take Mary as your wife, for the child conceived in her is from the Holy Spirit. She will bear a son, and you are to name him Jesus, for he will save his people from their sins." All this took place to fulfill what had been spoken by the Lord through the prophet:

> "Look, the virgin shall conceive and bear a son,
>   and they shall name him Emmanuel,"

which means, "God is with us." When Joseph awoke from sleep, he did as the angel of the Lord commanded him; he took her as his wife, but had no marital relations with her until she had borne a son; and he named him Jesus.

LUKE 2:1–20

In those days a decree went out from Emperor Augustus that all the world should be registered. This was the first registration and was taken while Quirinius was governor of Syria. All went to their own towns to be registered. Joseph also went from the town of Nazareth in Galilee to Judea, to the city of David called Bethlehem, because he was descended from the house and family of David. He went to be registered with Mary, to whom he was engaged and who was expecting a child. While they were there, the time came for her to deliver her child. And she gave birth to her firstborn son and wrapped him in bands of cloth, and laid him in a manger, because there was no place for them in the inn.

In that region there were shepherds living in the fields, keeping watch over their flock by night. Then an angel of the Lord stood before them, and the glory of the Lord shone around them, and they were terrified. But the angel said to them, "Do not be afraid; for see—I am bringing you good news of great joy for all the people: to you is born this day in the city of David a Savior, who is the Messiah, the Lord. This will be a sign for you: you will find a child wrapped in bands of cloth and lying in a manger." And suddenly there was with the angel a multitude of the heavenly host, praising God and saying,

> "Glory to God in the highest heaven,
>   and on earth peace among those whom he favors!"

When the angels had left them and gone into heaven, the shepherds said to one another, "Let us go now to Bethlehem and see this thing that has taken place, which the Lord has made known to us." So they went with haste and found Mary and Joseph, and the child lying in the manger. When they saw this, they made known what had been told them about this child; and all who heard it were amazed at what the shepherds told them. But Mary treasured all these words and pondered them in her heart. The shepherds returned, glorifying and praising God for all they had heard and seen, as it had been told them.

LUKE 2:22–39

When the time came for their purification according to the law of Moses, they brought him up to Jerusalem to present him to the Lord (as it is written in the law of the Lord, "Every firstborn male shall be designated as holy to the Lord"), and they offered a sacrifice according to what is stated in the law of the Lord, "a pair of turtledoves or two young pigeons."

Now there was a man in Jerusalem whose name was Simeon; this man was righteous and devout, looking forward to the consolation of Israel, and the Holy Spirit rested on him. It had been revealed to him by the Holy Spirit that he would not see death before he had seen the Lord's Messiah. Guided by the Spirit, Simeon came into the temple; and when the parents brought in the child Jesus, to do for him what was customary under the law, Simeon took him in his arms and praised God, saying, "Master, now you are dismissing your servant in peace, according to your word; for my eyes have seen your salvation, which you have prepared in the presence of all peoples, a light for revelation to the Gentiles and for glory to your people Israel."

And the child's father and mother were amazed at what was being said about him. Then Simeon blessed them and said to his mother Mary, "This child is destined for the falling and the rising of many in Israel, and to be a sign that will be opposed so that the inner thoughts of many will be revealed—and a sword will pierce your own soul too."

There was also a prophet, Anna the daughter of Phanuel, of the tribe of Asher. She was of a great age, having lived with her husband seven years after her marriage, then as a widow to the age of eighty-four. She never left the temple but worshiped there with fasting and prayer night and day. At that moment she came, and began to praise God and to speak about the child to all who were looking for the redemption of Jerusalem.

When they had finished everything required by the law of the Lord, they returned to Galilee, to their own town of Nazareth.

MATTHEW 2:11

On entering the house, the [Wise Men from the East] saw the child with Mary his mother; and they knelt down and paid him homage. Then, opening their treasure chests, they offered him gifts of gold, frankincense, and myrrh.

MATTHEW 2:13–15

An angel of the Lord appeared to Joseph in a dream and said, "Get up, take the child and his mother, and flee to Egypt, and remain there until I tell you; for Herod is about to search for the child, to destroy him." Then Joseph got up, took the child and his mother by night, and went to Egypt, and remained there until the death of Herod. This was to fulfill what had been spoken by the Lord through the prophet, "Out of Egypt I have called my son."

MATTHEW 2:19–21

Then Herod died, an angel of the Lord suddenly appeared in a dream to Joseph in Egypt and said, "Get up, take the child and his mother, and go to the land of Israel, for those who were seeking the child's life are dead." Then Joseph got up, took the child and his mother, and went to the land of Israel.

LUKE 2:41–51

Now every year his parents went to Jerusalem for the festival of the Passover. And when he was twelve years old, they went up as usual for the festival. When the festival was ended and they started to return, the boy Jesus stayed behind in Jerusalem, but his parents did not know it. Assuming that he was in the group of travelers, they went a day's journey. Then they started to look for him among their relatives and friends. When they did not find him, they returned to Jerusalem to search for him. After three days they found him in the temple, sitting among the teachers, listening to them and asking them questions. And all who heard him were amazed at his understanding and his answers. When his parents saw him they were astonished; and his mother said to him, "Child, why have you treated us like this? Look, your father and I have been searching for you in great anxiety." He said to them, "Why were you searching for me? Did you not know that I must be in my Father's house?" But they did not understand what he said to them. Then he went down with them and came to Nazareth, and was obedient to them. His mother treasured all these things in her heart.

JOHN 2:1–12

On the third day there was a wedding in Cana of Galilee, and the mother of Jesus was there. Jesus and his disciples had also been invited to the wedding. When the wine gave out, the mother of Jesus said to him, "They have no wine." And Jesus said to her, "Woman, what concern is that to you and to me? My hour has not yet come." His mother said to the servants, "Do whatever he tells you." Now standing there were six stone water jars for the Jewish rites of purification, each holding twenty or thirty gallons. Jesus said to them, "Fill the jars with water." And they filled them up to the brim. He said to them, "Now draw some out, and take it to the chief steward." So they took it. When the steward tasted the water that had become wine, and did not know where it came from (though the servants who had drawn the water

LUKE 2:25–32

Now there was a man in Jerusalem whose name was Simeon; this man was righteous and devout, looking forward to the consolation of Israel, and the Holy Spirit rested on him. It had been revealed to him by the Holy Spirit that he would not see death before he had seen the Lord's Messiah. Guided by the Spirit, Simeon came into the temple; and when the parents brought in the child Jesus, to do for him what was customary under the law, Simeon took him in his arms and praised God, saying,

> "Master, now you are dismissing your servant in peace,
>   according to your word;
> for my eyes have seen your salvation,
>   which you have prepared in the presence of all peoples,
> a light for revelation to the Gentiles
>   and for glory to your people Israel."

LEVITICUS 12:6–7

When the days of her purification are completed, whether for a son or for a daughter, she shall bring to the priest at the entrance of the tent of meeting a lamb in its first year for a burnt offering, and a pigeon or a turtledove for a sin offering. He shall offer it before the LORD, and make atonement on her behalf; then she shall be clean from her flow of blood. This is the law for her who bears a child, male or female.

JOHN 8:12

Jesus spoke to them, saying, "I am the light of the world. Whoever follows me will never walk in darkness but will have the light of life."

1.9 Safely in Her Arms

MATTHEW 2:13–15

Now after the wise men had left, an angel of the Lord appeared to Joseph in a dream and said, "Get up, take the child and his mother, and flee to Egypt, and remain there until I tell you; for Herod is about to search for the child, to destroy him." Then Joseph got up, took the child and his mother by night, and went to Egypt, and remained there until the death of Herod. This was to fulfill what had been spoken by the Lord through the prophet, "Out of Egypt I have called my son."

1.10 A Mother's Influence

JOHN 2:1–11.

See page 169.

Chapter Two
MARY, MOTHER OF GOD

2.1 Introduction

REVELATION 19:16

On his robe and on his thigh he has a name inscribed, "King of kings and Lord of lords."

2.3 Mary, the Throne of God's Wisdom

I KINGS 10:18–20

The king also made a great ivory throne, and overlaid it with the finest gold. The throne had six steps. The top of the throne was rounded in the back, and on each side of the seat were arm rests and two lions standing beside the arm rests, while twelve lions were standing, one on each end of a step on the six steps. Nothing like it was ever made in any kingdom.

2.8 Royalty Meets Royalty

MATTHEW 2:1–2

Wise men from the East came to Jerusalem, asking, "Where is the child who has been born king of the Jews? For we observed his star at its rising, and have come to pay him homage."

PSALM 72:10–11

May the kings of Tarshish and of the isles render him.

ISAIAH 60:3

Nations shall come to your light, and kings to the brightness of your dawn.

MATTHEW 2:9

When [the Magi] had heard the king [Herod], they set out; and there, ahead of them, went the star that they had seen at its rising, until it stopped over the place where the child was.

2.10 Beloved Mother and Child
Latin inscription in the window: O(MN)IS VALLIS I(M)PLEBITUR

LUKE 3:5

Every valley shall be filled,
  and every mountain and hill shall be made low.

ISAIAH 40:4

Every valley shall be lifted up,
  and every mountain and hill be made low.

Chapter Three
MARY, MOTHER OF THE CHURCH

3.2 Jesus's Commissioning of Mary

JOHN 19:29

A jar full of sour wine was standing there. So they put a sponge full of the wine on a branch of hyssop and held it to his mouth.

JOHN 19:34

One of the soldiers pierced his side with a spear, and at once blood and water came out.

3.3 Mary at the Empty Tomb

MARK 16:1–5

When the sabbath was over, Mary Magdalene, and Mary the mother of James, and Salome bought spices, so that they might go and anoint him. And very early on the first day of the week, when the sun had risen, they went to the tomb. They had been saying to one another, "Who will roll away the stone for us from the entrance to the tomb?" When they looked up, they saw that the stone, which was very large, had already been rolled back. As they entered the tomb, they saw a young man, dressed in a white robe, sitting on the right side; and they were alarmed.

MATTHEW 28:4

For fear of [the angel] the guards shook and became like dead men.

JOHN 20:5–6

[The disciple] bent down to look in and saw the linen wrappings lying there, but he did not go in. Then Simon Peter came, following him, and went into the tomb. He saw the linen wrappings lying there.

3.9 Mary, the Intermediary to the Son of God

I JOHN 2:1–2

My little children, I am writing these things to you so that you may not sin. But if anyone does sin, we have an advocate with the Father, Jesus Christ the righteous; and he is the atoning sacrifice for our sins, and not for ours only but also for the sins of the whole world.

Chapter Four
MARY, MOTHER OF US ALL

4.4 Mary's Advice

JOHN 2:1–11.

See pages 169–170.

4.10 Sharing the Joy and Grief of Motherhood

LUKE 1:39–56.

See pages 163–164.

MATTHEW 3:1–3

In those days John the Baptist appeared in the wilderness of Judea, proclaiming, "Repent, for the kingdom of heaven has come near." This is the one of whom the prophet Isaiah spoke when he said,

"The voice of one crying out in the wilderness:
'Prepare the way of the Lord,
make his paths straight.'"

ISAIAH 40:3

A voice cries out:
"In the wilderness prepare the way of the Lord,
make straight in the desert a highway for our God.

LUKE 2:8–11

In that region [Judea] there were shepherds living in the fields, keeping watch over their flock by night. Then an angel of the Lord stood before them, and the glory of the Lord shone around them, and they were terrified. But the angel said to them, "Do not be afraid; for see—I am bringing you good news of great joy for all the people: to you is born this day in the city of David a Savior, who is the Messiah, the Lord.

Chapter Five:
MARY AT CHARTRES IN THE
TWENTY-FIRST CENTURY

5.2 Mary, Mother of the Son of Justice

GENESIS 3:15

I will put enmity between you [the serpent] and the woman,
      and between your offspring and hers;
he will strike your head,
      and you will strike his heel.

Note: Early Vulgate (Latin) and Coptic (Egyptian) translations mistakenly translated the end of the verse, "She will strike your head."

5.3 Mary, a Mother Who Has Suffered

MATTHEW 2:16–18

When [King] Herod saw that he had been tricked by the wise men, he was infuriated, and he sent and killed all the children in and around Bethlehem who were two years old or under, according to the time that he had learned from the wise men. Then was fulfilled what had been spoken through the prophet Jeremiah:

"A voice was heard in Ramah,
    wailing and loud lamentation,
Rachel weeping for her children;
    she refused to be consoled because they are no more."

INDEX OF BIBLICAL CITATIONS

Old Testament

New Testament

INDEX OF PERSONS

INDEX OF SUBJECTS

ABOUT PARACLETE PRESS

WHO WE ARE

Paraclete Press is a publisher of books, recordings, and DVDs on Christian spirituality. Our publishing represents a full expression of Christian belief and practice—from Catholic to Evangelical, from Protestant to Orthodox.

We are the publishing arm of the Community of Jesus, an ecumenical monastic community in the Benedictine tradition. As such, we are uniquely positioned in the marketplace without connection to a large corporation and with informal relationships to many branches and denominations of faith.

WHAT WE ARE DOING

Paraclete Press Books

Paraclete publishes books that show the richness and depth of what it means to be Christian. Although Benedictine spirituality is at the heart of who we are and all that we do, we publish books that reflect the Christian experience across many cultures, time periods, and houses of worship. We publish books that nourish the vibrant life of the church and its people.

We have several different series, including the best-selling Paraclete Essentials and Paraclete Giants series of classic texts in contemporary English; Voices from the Monastery—men and women monastics writing about living a spiritual life today; our award-winning Paraclete Poetry series as well as the Mount Tabor Books on the arts; best-selling gift books for children on the occasions of baptism and first communion; and the Active Prayer Series that brings creativity and liveliness to any life of prayer.

Mount Tabor Books

Paraclete's newest series, Mount Tabor Books, focuses on the arts and literature as well as liturgical worship and spirituality, and was created in conjunction with the Mount Tabor Ecumenical Centre for Art and Spirituality in Barga, Italy.

Paraclete Records

From Gregorian chant to contemporary American choral works, our recordings celebrate the best of sacred choral music composed through the centuries that create a space for heaven and earth to intersect. Paraclete Recordings is the record label representing the internationally acclaimed choir Gloriæ Dei Cantores, praised for their "rapt and fathomless spiritual intensity" by *American Record Guide*; the Gloriæ Dei Cantores Schola, specializing in the study and performance of Gregorian chant; and the other instrumental artists of the Arts Empowering Life Foundation.

Paraclete Press is also privileged to be the exclusive North American distributor of the recordings of the Monastic Choir of St. Peter's Abbey in Solesmes, France, long considered to be a leading authority on Gregorian chant.

Paraclete Video Productions

Our DVDs offer spiritual help, healing, and biblical guidance for a broad range of life issues including grief and loss, marriage, forgiveness, facing death, bullying, addictions, Alzheimer's, and spiritual formation.

SCAN
TO
READ
MORE

Learn more about us at our website
WWW.PARACLETEPRESS.COM
In the USA phone us toll-free at 1.800.451.5006;
outside the USA phone us at +1.508.255.4685